*The Book of*

# WEST HUNTSPILL

## *A Millennium Celebration*

*Compiled by*

## THE PARISH COMMUNITY

HALSGROVE

First published in Great Britain in 2001

Frontispiece photograph: *Jack Baker and Mr Spickett's leather shop, 1920s.*

**British Library Cataloguing-in-Publication Data**
A CIP record for this title is available from the British Library

ISBN 1 84114 108 9

**HALSGROVE**
PUBLISHING, MEDIA AND DISTRIBUTION

Halsgrove House
Lower Moor Way
Tiverton, Devon EX16 6SS
Tel: 01884 243242
Fax: 01884 243325
email: sales@halsgrove.com
website:  www.halsgrove.com

Printed and bound in Great Britain by Bookcraft Ltd., Midsomer Norton

*Whilst every care has been taken to ensure the accuracy of the
information contained in this book, the author disclaims responsibility
for any mistakes which may have inadvertently been included.*

# Dedication

*This book is dedicated to the memory of
Mrs J.A.K. Tiley –'Jen' to one and all,
a true servant of the community
which she loved so dearly.*

*Strawberry picking at Swell House in the early 1960s.*

# FOREWORD

West Huntspill has been alluded to in many historical and literary works over the years. There have been a number of works produced locally by such bodies as the WI, in 1953, and for specific occasions, such as the school centenary in 1997. The *Parish Magazine*, which reflects the pattern of village life, has also been a sounding board for short historical articles.

The production of this book was begun as part of the Millennium Project, instigated by the Parish Council in 1998. It is not an exhaustive history. However, it has been a community effort. The basic historical record has been provided by an authoritative amateur, well respected in historical and archaeological circles. Most of the remaining contributions, including photographs and documents, have been provided by the members of clubs, societies and associations within the parish, bodies that form the fabric of a village community. Some members of extended village families have also been brave enough to put pen to paper to disclose their family histories and recollections.

What has resulted must, of course, be only the tip of the iceberg of the historical data available. Much remains unrecorded, but it is hoped that there will be much to enjoy on the following pages.

*Colin Hall*,
Chairman of West Huntspill Parish Council,
June 2001.

*John Allum waiting to receive his coronation Bible from Reverend Morgan, Raymond Dean and the Chairman of West Huntspill Parish Council Mr W.C. Parkhouse, June 1953.*

*Leekbeds Drove.*

*Pawlett Road before it was bypassed by the main road in 1926.*

# ACKNOWLEDGEMENTS

The compilation of a book such as this will make very little progress if it cannot draw on source material. To this end the project has been well served. Thanks must go to:

Madge Langdon for her historical research, narrative and material, which has been invaluable; the *Huntspill News* for permission to quote from various articles; Enid Bryant for her contributions on Sealey's Farm, Joanna Martin and Samuel Taylor Coleridge; West Huntspill CP School for loan of the School Log and Punishment Register; Pete Derham and Graham Saunders for their families' contributions; David Holley for Harvest Home and Harvest Supper information; Betty Lambert for Welfare Clinic and Steam Railway Club information; the Loud family for Alstone Court information; and Janet O'Neill for part of the Court Farm contribution. We thank the Somerset Archaeological and Natural History Society for survey reports on Sealey's Farm and 5/7 Silver Street and the Somerset Record Office for permission to reproduce the 1840 Tithe Map.

Photography is a major part of this book and thanks must also go to those that have given permission to reproduce various photographs: The Burnham and Highbridge *Mercury/Weekly News*, Mike Long (an independent photographer) of Burnham-on-Sea, the Somerset Archaeological and Natural History Society for 'North-east view of Huntspill Church, 1843' by John Buckler, and the *Weston Mercury*. Most other sources have been identified within the text where possible.

A special thanks to all members of the community, clubs and societies who have supplied contributions, information, documents and photographs. There has been one request for anonymity, which has been adhered to, but it would have been difficult to complete the book without that person's invaluable help.

*Milestone on the A38*
*near the primary school.*

*Pump on the Common.  There is a second pump on New Road opposite the school.*

# CONTENTS

*Porch House in the 1860s.*

*Ringstone children's street party, summer 1970, with Bill Shiels in the foreground.*

*Cherry trees in the churchyard.*

*Chapter One*

# WEST HUNTSPILL
# THROUGH THE CENTURIES

*May the sea-wall stand ever still*
*And guard us all who live at Huntspill*
Old Huntspill motto

West Huntspill is situated on the Somerset Levels, approximately five miles north of Bridgwater and three miles from Burnham-on-Sea. The village lies on either side of the A38, close to the M5 motorway. Approximately half a mile of farmland separates it from the estuary of the Parrett to the west. It occupies a slightly raised bed of Burtle sand and gravel extending from the Huntspill River in the south to the River Brue at Highbridge in the north. A sea wall, reconstructed after the disastrous flood of 1982, borders the east bank of the River Parrett. The main drainage, the Cadwells Rhyne and North Rhyne, run eastwards from the village to empty into the River Brue. The raised ground and the varied soil types have combined to produce valuable farmland. Cattle and sheep are the mainstay of the farms; there is now little ploughland and few apple orchards, and the cider orchards, many of which are shown on the Tithe records of 1840, have gone. Records show a wide variety of crops being grown in earlier centuries. In 1845, for example, it was reported that a flood destroyed crops of wheat, vetches and winter oats.

Throughout the Middle Ages, however, the main economic 'crop' in West Huntspill, in common with many other parts of the country, was wool. Wool and cloth were exported through Bridgwater bringing rich rewards for the lords of the manor and other local tradesmen. The church at Huntspill, notably the nave, chancel and later the tower, were built in the 14th, 15th and early-16th centuries respectively, with funds raised through the lucrative woollen trade. In this West Huntspill was no exception and it is a well-known saying that the churches and fine Somerset towers were 'built on the backs of the sheep'.

West Huntspill is a pleasant rural parish, containing principally those who commute to local towns to work, retired persons and schoolchildren. There is a Post Office Stores, as well as a garage and no less than six inns and restaurants along the A38. New housing estates have been built and the population has increased in recent years.

Evidence of early human activity has been found in many parts of the village. A sandy shore and fertile soil, coupled with the existence of an established route along the coast of the Bristol Channel from the Mendip Hills to Pawlett Hill and the Parrett estuary, must have been attractive to

Top: *An Iron-Age (Lake Village type) bowl,*
*in black burnished pottery, found at an excavation*
*in 1993 at Alstone.*

Bottom: *The excavation at Alstone. The occupation*
*(on a raised Burtle bed near the sea) was 1st century* BC
*or 1st century* AD. *A farm site, it was bordered by a*
*ditch which was filled with rubbish; broken pot, ash,*
*bones of cattle and sheep, also horse, pig and dog.*
*Traces of occupation were also found in c.1962 and*
*reported in* Somerset Archaeological and Natural
History Society Proceedings *No.113, 1967.*

*Church Road near the church during the flood of 1903.*

*Church Road (then Poorhouse Lane) during the flood of 1903.*

hunters and early farmers arriving in the area. Neolithic and Bronze-Age flint implements have been found and Iron-Age people, who used the 'Glastonbury' style of pottery, are known to have lived at Alstone and kept domestic animals, cattle, sheep, horses and dogs. In the main village pottery dating from the 1st–4th centuries AD and traces of simple wooden buildings with timber slot foundations, hearths and cobbled floors indicate a considerable spread of population (which, in fact, continued northwards into the Burnham area and along the Polden Hills). In common with most parts of the West Country, evidence of activity in this village is sadly lacking after the Roman occupation ended and the Dark Ages began. We next hear about Huntspill, or the 'Manor of Honespulle', in a deed of AD787 by which time the Saxons had reached the Parrett and Offa was King of Mercia. A manorial holding was obviously in existence and the people were Christian. The deed gave the lands of the manor and five hides of land to the Abbey at Glastonbury. Glastonbury continued to hold this land until the Norman Conquest, when the manors of Huntspill and Alstone were granted by William the Conqueror to Walter de Douai (who also held other manors, perhaps as a reward for his loyalty to the King). What happened to Alwin (son of Goda) and Alwaker, the Saxons who held the lands before, is not recorded, but the small hamlet of Withy continued to be held by Glastonbury until the Reformation.

The Domesday Book of 1086 lists land for 16 ploughs, 23 villagers, 6 smallholders, 7 cottagers and 4 slaves, as well as 100 acres of meadow, 20 mares, 200 acres of pasture, 20 cattle, 38 pigs and 108 sheep – all valued at £9. The manor of Alstone (Alsistone) was also given to Walter de Douai and rented to Waldema. This was a smaller settlement with land for 3 ploughs, 1 villager and 4 smallholders, incorporating 40 acres of pasture, 10 cattle, 19 pigs and 45 sheep. The manors were reputed to comprise the richest and best land in the area. During the Middle Ages the land was divided into a number of manors sometimes leased to the main manor which was held by the Cogan family from 1280 to 1389. They were very wealthy and are thought to have been responsible for the building of the main part of the church. The effigies of one of them (either Richard, who died in 1386, or William, who died in 1382), together with their wives, can be seen in the wall of the nave.

Of the medieval village we have a few traces and clues. Unglazed pottery shards have been found in the soil in the areas of Grove Farm, the church, the Common and along Church Road. The wood-and-thatch cottages of the villagers leave little trace. A hollow way and house platforms can be seen in the large field west of Grove Farm (which was thought both by Collinson in 1790 and the curate Revd Bennett in his 1875 History of Huntspill to be the site

of Cogan Manor). The site of the present farm was at one time partially encircled by the old course of the Cadwells Rhyne and a deep depression runs along the west side of the site. This part of the village is not seen on maps of the 16th century onwards. The village in the 15th and 16th centuries appears to have run along the Common, Silver Street, Cadwells Lane and Cadwells Drove. But the houses along the Cadwells were swept away by the flood of 1607 with the loss of 28 lives. This risk of flooding has always been high because of the proximity of the estuary of the Parrett, and more floods are recorded in 1704, 1710, 1790, 1890, 1902 and 1911, with the last one in 1982. The village, on an exposed coast, was, and still is, affected by wind and storms. Court Rolls record a storm in November 1836 when many old trees were blown down. The then rector Noel Ellison purchased replacements – many of the fine beeches, limes and other trees now in the churchyard date from this time. The maintenance of the sea wall and coastal defences has been a subject of importance – and controversy – throughout the history of the village. In 1790 the seashore was described as consisting of large sand dunes. Fishing was carried on along the sea wall and various fishermen are mentioned (one in particular in 1828) as living in a cottage built at the eastern end of the graveyard. This cottage was later purchased and demolished by the Revd Noel Ellison to make way for the schoolroom (where today a stone section from the old wall incorporated in the west wall of the building can still be seen).

The course of the Parrett has changed on many occasions. In an article entitled 'Memoirs of the Geological Survey' published in 1876, Woodward described the then recent changes in the course of the lower Parrett. In 1739, for example, the river was blocked by ice which caused deposition and this in turn blocked the channel. As a result an island called Dunball Island became joined to Huntspill. Evidence of this event remains to this day. Part of the land south of the Huntspill River is still called 'The Island' and Mr W. Parkhouse, an old resident, described to the compilers of this volume how the flood of 1911 reached the A38 and swept away a farmhouse in the area near the river, shown as 'The Island' on the 1840 Tithe Map.

The 'Auster' system placed responsibility for the maintenance of the sea wall on the occupiers of land which lay along its length and stones marked with initials indicating the appropriate landowners have been incorporated in the new wall. Disputes inevitably occurred and landholders were blamed for neglect on many occasions. Part of the west bank of the Parrett is still, officially, in the ecclesiastical Parish of Huntspill. Cattle were taken from Steart to Steart Island for grazing at low tide and the three-field system was kept in operation until the 18th century and the Enclosure Acts. Northfield, where the Northfield Rhyne runs south of Alstone, Westfield (or 'Middle Field' on Locke's map of 1770) near Plymor Farm, and Southfield just south of the church all indicate the old 'common' fields. From the top of the church tower, in the right light, traces of the strip system – ridge and furrow – can be seen on the field to the south.

Vestry Books held at the Record Office, Court Rolls and the Bishop's Court at Wells reflect events in the village – among the more dramatic at least one murder – these being principally disputes over waterways and the blocking of the same, resulting in flooding and disputes between landholders. Repairs to the roads are also reported.

Before the Enclosure Acts, the low-lying moors provided summer grazing for cattle and sheep and areas were allocated to the different villages. For example, at Huntspill Moor, north of Woolavington and Puriton, cattle were also taken across the Parrett to graze at Steart. The 'Warths' along the Brue, still marked near Alstone, were areas embanked with stones and withies along the river to catch the mud and increase the area of land. The village must have been affected by the plague (the Black Death) in 1349 but not, it is thought, to the same great extent as many other places. It has been suggested that the large, fine church was built in the later part of the 14th century as an offering of thanks for the end of the plague years and returning prosperity.

Houses dating in part from the 14th and 15th centuries remain; Sealey's Farm on the Common and two houses, part of an original farm, near the church at Silver Street. Houses of probable 17th- and 18th-century origin include Porch House, Trivetts Farm, Guys Farm and part of the present Orchard Inn, which was the old Parish Poorhouse adjoining the Parish Pound (that part of Church Road was originally called 'Poorhouse Lane'). The Old Rectory is reported to have been largely rebuilt in 1710 by Revd J. Tripp, having been partially destroyed by fire. Mill Green Close was the site of a mill from medieval times and it is thought that the Leekbeds Rhyne which originally ran close to the northern part of Church Road was diverted at some date prior to the building of The Grange to a new straight channel through sandy ground to the site of the mill. The early course of the Cadwells Rhyne ran along the west side of the present A38 to the mill site; it was diverted at some date to cross under the road to the east near the Methodist Chapel. The mill and the houses attached were demolished in 1963 to make way for houses. A photograph taken during the demolition shows a large arched structure, possibly an oven.

The main A38, passing through what was once Smurl Common, was shown by Ogilvy on his road map of 1675 as a turnpike which passed through unfenced land with a windmill. An old milestone can be seen near New Road. Another mill, probably a 'post mill' worked by wind power, was also marked on that map in a field just south of the Crossways Inn. There is a theory that the route through the village before the Turnpike Acts may

*The Crossways and Main Road, early 1920s.*

have been Church Road, which winds around old farms leading towards the church and along the Common, largely across sandy ground where shards of 14th- and 15th-century pottery have been found. Long before that it seems probable that a route along the sand, avoiding the moors, led from Brean Down through Brean, Berrow, Burnham and Alstone, to a path which can still be traced across the fields by Maundrils Farm, across the large field by Grove Farm (the hollow way) along the church path past the church to Sloway on to Stretcholt – all on sandy ground yielding Roman and pre-Roman finds – to Pawlett Hill, then across to the old ferry at Combwich and onwards. Drainage and reclamation of the low-lying land continued; the disputes about the use of rhynes, dams, etc. are reported in the Wells Records.

In the years following the plague and the Peasants' Revolt the manorial system began to break down. After the line of the Cogans died out the manor passed through marriage and sale to many holders and the land was sold to tenants. There were, however, still areas of common land existing at 1777; at Huntspill (the present Common, where fairs were held), Smurl, Westhill and East Huntspill, as shown on a property map drawn by the local surveyor Mr Locke and held in the Record Office. This shows the effect of the break-up of the estates, with a profusion of separate plots and the names of their owners; Sealey (Sealey's Farm), Jeffery, Saunders, Popham, Jeanes and Gould being among those noted.

Improvements in agricultural methods led to prosperity – for some. The prosperity of the Bridgwater traders, for example, is apparent from their holdings, and their names in the church and school records indicate an interest in the village. During the 17th and 18th centuries Huntspill was reported to have been a fairly prosperous village with good agricultural land and numerous markets and fairs being held on the Common and at Highbridge. However, the disastrous flood of 1607 must have been a terrible experience – 28 people in the village were drowned and the houses along the Cadwells, probably only of wood and daub constructions, were abandoned. The village moved to slightly higher land, probably around Silver Street, near the church and along the main road. In effect it seems that the village moved eastwards – which may account for the location of the church today on the westward extremity of the settlement. A further flood is reported a century later when, as recorded in *Somerset & Dorset Notes and Queries*:

*... on the 27th of December about four of the clock in the morning a mighty Southwest wind blew so strong and strangely tore at the Sea Walls [that] ships [were] blown inshore.*

Huntspill was one of the first parishes to commence its Parish Records under the law of Elizabeth I. These are now held at the Somerset Record Office. There must have been great excitement at the time of the Armada but there is no record of this. During the Civil War Bridgwater and Taunton were heavily involved when Cromwell besieged the Castle and burned down much of the town. Huntspill was perhaps lucky to escape relatively unscathed.

Not so in 1685! Some 15 men of Huntspill are mentioned as having been involved in the Monmouth Rebellion. They are as follows: John Bindon of Alstone, Francis Came (who was tried at Taunton and died at sea on the way to Barbados), John Coombe (who was tried at Taunton and possibly hanged at Langport), John Foyle of Alstone, John Harris (who was transported to Barbados), Richard Harris (who was hanged), William Hooper, Ralph Howell, Thomas Hurford (who was hanged), John Leaker (who was transported to Barbados), John Long of Alstone, John Paine of Alstone, Thomas Palmer of Alstone Morris (who was later pardoned), John Pryor (who was transported to Barbados) and John Turner of Alstone. It is not clear what happened to many of these men.

This was a time of religious strife. Huntspill has reports of 'Recusants' who were fined for not attending church, among them Humphrey Grove (alias Seller), Ruth Grove, Agnes (wife of James Pike), yeoman Thomas Goulde and his wife, spinster Susanna Goulde (sic) and Humphrey Green. An event deemed worthy of note on 17 August 1619 was that Christopher Theare came into the church at Huntspill and sat near the pulpit with his hat on his head – and refused to take it off. After the seats were placed in church, special pews were allocated to local families and disputes occurred when others sat in their place. A Mr Charles Hawkins, for example, 'who is himself in possession of an ancient accustomed seat... has of late more than once lowered himself into the pew of Mr William Saunders.'

With reference to the enclosures of the 17th and 18th centuries, there is a sketchy but interesting series of road maps made by Ogilvy in 1675 (rather like the modern AA maps) which show the main layout of Huntspill. People were beginning to move about more and trade routes and communications networks were improving. Whatever the disputes, the appearance in the village of the very fine Royal Coat of Arms, ordered by Charles II on his return in 1660, indicates a willingness within Huntspill to accept the new regime – or a desire to appear to do so. By the 18th century the land was divided into separate plots and the old common fields had gone, although some of the Commons remained. The property map drawn up by John Locke in 1770 details the fields and their owners. Some of the names still remain in the village, including Saunders, Sealey (a Bridgwater merchant), Jeffery, Turner and

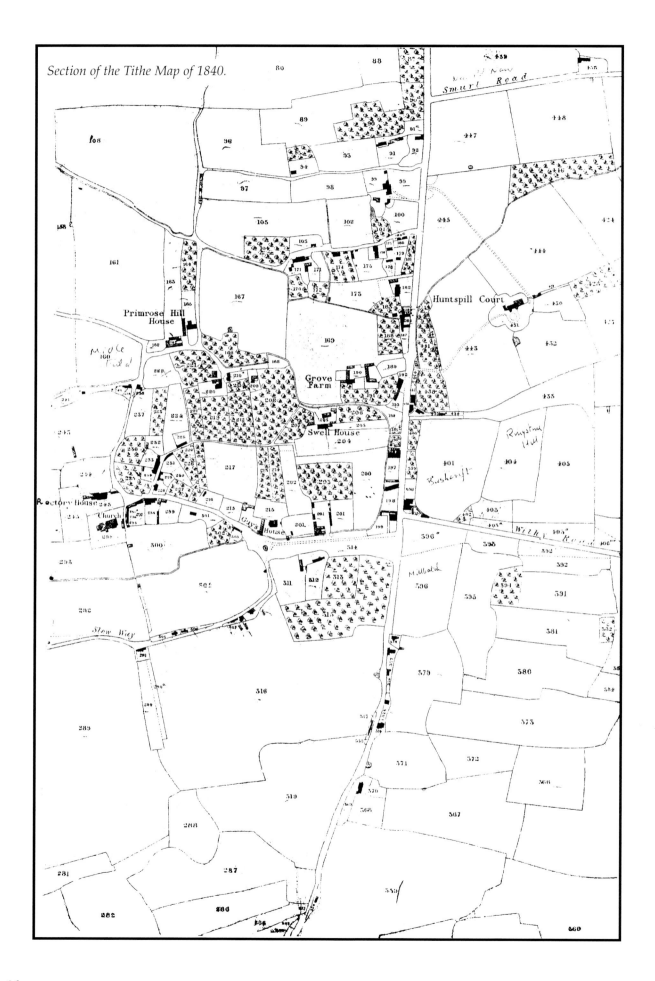

*Section of the Tithe Map of 1840.*

Came. John Locke was a pioneer in the improvement of land and influential during the Drainage Acts (the Huntspill Moor Act of 1774 and the 1801 Act for the New Cut and Clyce on the Brue). Although a number of Commons still existed at 1770 (Smurl, Westhill, Hackney and Heath Common), only the 'Fair Field', now known as the Common, remained when the Tithe Maps were drawn in 1840. The Enclosure Acts of the 18th century had deprived the poor tenants, with perhaps the odd cow or pig, of their grazing rights, and great poverty ensued.

By the time of the 1840 Tithe Map the village has assumed its present shape, although of course with far fewer houses. Places shown were Alstone Court, the old house next to the Artillery Inn, Maundrils Farm, New House Farm, the present Sundowner Café, the Poorhouse (now the Orchard Inn) and adjoining Parish Pound, The Grange, Huntspill Court, Primrose Hill House (now Plymor Farm), Swell House, The Poplars, Trivetts Farm, Grove Farm, houses on the west side of Silver Street, cottages and the schoolhouse near the church, the church itself, the Rectory, Guy's House and Sealey's Farm. Interestingly, the map shows a building in the field immediately north of the Rectory wood said to be the site of the Tithe Barn. Details of the owners and tenants of the plots shown on the Tithe are given in a schedule held at the Record Office.

Of particular note is the number of orchards on the map. During the 17th and 18th centuries a more prosperous agriculture (referred to by Collinson in his *History of Somerset* of 1791 when he described Huntspill as having 140 houses and 750 inhabitants with wealthy graziers, rich pasture and meadow) and an interest in machinery and draining land led to the drainage and enclosure of the Moors. There are some Enclosure Awards for Huntspill dated 1782. The enclosure of roadside strips may be seen still by houses along the road accompanied by long, narrow pieces of land.

The number of Commons still existing at 1770 is shown on Locke's map of that date. There is no road shown where New Road is (although it was in place, and named Smurl Road, by 1840), but Smurl Common is shown on the east side of the A38 where the School and Smurl Lane are now. North of Newbridge is Westhill Common, and to the east are Hackney Common and Heath Common. An open area up Leekbeds Lane is called simply 'Leekbeds'. Local historians since Bennett have been baffled by the name of this thoroughfare. Leekbeds is an old Somerset word meaning 'a broad, leek-green swamp'. Interestingly, on Locke's map there was an area of mud, which was later reclaimed, known as the 'North' and 'Great Slime Batches', which appear to be where the present saltings and sea wall are. Huntspill Common, the site of a fair held on 19 June, is also noted on the map – the only Common remaining.

# Joanna of Huntspill

Joanna Martin was illegitimate, 'the fruit of illicit commerce', as the Reverend Warner, author, wrote in 1800. In 1736 her mother had given birth in the Poorhouse (now the Orchard Inn) and disappeared leaving her baby the property of nobody. Joanna received no education, and at the age of 12 was sent into service in Huntspill passing from one master to another as 'a sort fixture or heirloom, without inquiry or regard'. Her wardrobe on leaving the Poorhouse was one ragged gown. Eventually Joanna married a labourer named Gould, but, according to her own verbal account, 'took terribly to breeding', and produced seven children in seven years. While she was big with her eighth it 'pleased Providence to take her husband from her'. Now she was a widow with six children (two had died) and no money. Joanna applied for relief to parish officers, but was told that whilst there was no relief for 'Out paupers', the children were welcome in the Poorhouse. Remembering her own experiences Joanna swiftly declined. Not to be beaten, she began to rise at 2a.m., do chores, then walk up to ten miles to market with a basket of her own which she made by hand and earthenware pottery on her head. She also sold rags. By this 'horse-like labour' she saved a guinea and a half in a year.

But fate dealt another blow. Having been evicted from her cottage Joanna resolved to build her own. Buying materials she set to, but soon found it too difficult a task for one person. She hired an assistant but unfortunately this hireling discovered Joanna's savings hidden in a rag. The villain quickly decamped, taking the money and some of the building materials with him. This latest setback was retrospectively met with the comment: 'I did curse the rascal, but I had not leisure to grieve. I determined to work harder than ever to provide for my children.' Joanna left the cottage half built and, together with her six children with whom she shared one bed, slept in the shell of the building with only the dew board (planks) for cover instead of a roof. Joanna finally finished her cottage and took pride in furnishing it herself. Her activities and stoicism caused a stir in Huntspill and she soon found another husband whose surname, Martin, she took. Joanna became a happy woman who sang with a fine voice and who cracked the whip as she drove her little pony and cart to market. Her legs had started to give out and a 30-mile walk had become rather daunting. The pottery and rag trade prospered, Joanna buried her second husband, married a third called Pain and amassed a small fortune of several hundred pounds.

This shrewd and energetic woman was beholden to no one. Now a celebrity in the village, she lived at Bats Bow, New Road, in a house owned by a local dignitary named Thomas Jennings.

Having buried her third husband the merry widow saw her children grow and flourish. She told the itinerant Revd Warner, 'I don't give a farthing for the Pope or Caesar', providing us with a rare glimpse into the finer details of her character. As Thomas Jennings wrote:

*Had she been more favourably thrown, had she been in a sphere where her original talents and energies could have been improved by education, her name might have have been added to a list of distinguished female worthies of this country.*

And, indeed, if this were the case we would no doubt today know far more of this remarkable woman.

# HUNTSPILL'S MARITIME CONNECTIONS

The contemporaries Naval Commander Charles Came, Admiral Sir Charles Saunders and Captain James Cook all had a connection with Huntspill, (although the latter's association is rather tenuous having been discounted by the James Cook Museum at Whitby, but authenticated by research undertaken in the early 1900s by a family descendant).

Charles Came was born in 1770, the son of William Came of Plymor Hill House as the farm was called in those days. One of Charles' Godfathers was a relative of his grandfather and, being a Lord High Admiral, gave his Godson an appointment in the Navy. In 1793 Charles went to the West Indies and showed such bravery that he was made a Post Captain when just 24 years of age. As a Lieutenant he commanded a sloop captured from the French and, after his promotion to Commander, was posted to the *Grampus*, one of the vessels caught up in the great naval mutiny at the Nore in 1797. Following this the vessel, a storeship converted to a '4th rate' ship (meaning it carried 50 guns), sailed to the West Indies where Charles died of yellow fever at the age of 27.

According to the biographer of Charles Saunders, his family had lived in Huntspill in a house known as Saunders' Court. This would have been Huntspill Court where the Saunders are known to have been living during the early decades of the 18th century. Charles was born c.1713, but his place of birth is not known. James, his father, was church-warden here for a time and, on his death, bequeathed an endowment for the poor which is recorded on one of the charity boards at the back of the church. Charles entered the Navy around 1727 and, in 1740, was a First Lieutenant on the *Centurion*, the vessel that carried Anson on his famous voyage around the world which took almost four years.

Charles Saunders saw action in the Mediterranean, during which time many French prizes were taken, and for a while entered Parliament. He was knighted and appointed an Admiral and, as such, commanded the expedition, with Wolfe and an Army contingent aboard, which led to the capture of Quebec in 1759. The remaining 16 years of his life saw him again capturing French vessels, serving as a Member of Parliament and being made First Lord of the Admiralty and a Privy Councillor in Pitt's Government of 1766.

*Huntspill Court, 1920s.*

William Came, a brother of the aforementioned Charles Came, left Huntspill after the death of his father in 1785 and went to live in Bridgwater. In 1787 he married Ann Cook, who was a niece of the celebrated Captain James Cook and who brought with her into the Came family books and items belonging to her uncle. William Came's marriage to this girl should not seem so very surprising for James Cook sailed with Charles Saunders on the *Anson* expedition and William's brother Charles was also a naval man of note. Thus the paths of all three could well have crossed at some stage.

Earlier items of note in relation to Huntspill's maritime connections include a dispute which took place as far back as 1242 between various merchants of Bristol concerning a ship which was lying at Huntspill. This must be one of the earliest references to a wharf, or landing stage, here. In 1361 a special licence was granted to the Rector of Huntspill authorising him to ship the produce grown on Church land across to Wales and sell it for his own profit. During the 1540s the merchants of Bridgwater wrote concerning their apprehension about goods coming by water to Huntspill taking trade away from themselves. In 1548 a Venetian trading vessel was wrecked on the sea wall at Huntspill, and in 1673 Court records included the comment: 'Diverse Irish cattle both sheep and oxen have been landed in the Parish of Huntspill illegally.'

After the severe storm of 1703, John Tripp, the local rector, wrote to Daniel Defoe relating the misfortune of five vessels belonging to Bridgwater quay which had been driven by a violent sea 'out of the Channel upon a wharf in OUR parish which lay some distance off from the Channel.'

A reference in the local burial register concerning the funeral of Ann Rice in 1834 mentions that she had been killed on the 'Huntspill Coal Wharf', which was probably on the south side of the River Brue, on the bank opposite the site where Highbridge Wharf was later constructed and perhaps in the immediate vicinity of the wharf referred to by John Tripp over a century earlier. During the 1830s and '40s the bulk of the area behind the Highbridge Inn and to the west, bounded by the river and the Clyce, was a large brickyard, ideally placed for transporting the finished product by boat. A report in the local press from 1866 refers to an accident which befell a craft 'engaged in its daily occupation of conveying grist from Steart to the Huntspill seawall'. Grist probably constituted small stones or pebbles and the implication is that this carriage had been taking place for a long time. In the same year an old man drowned when his boat 'heavily laden with bricks and slabs of wood' keeled over in the River Brue near Bason Bridge whilst heading from Highbridge to Tadham Moor – the bricks and wood would have been transhipped from vessels calling at the Highbridge wharf.

Five or six residents from Huntspill appear in the list of shipowners connected with the port of Bridgwater during the 19th century. Several are from a long line of fishing families, while another, listed as a coal merchant, was the owner of the brickyard behind the Highbridge Inn. Bath bricks were produced there, indicating that the industry was not solely confined to Bridgwater. This latter person owned a vessel named the *Gannet* which was built at Neath in 1825 and traded for him from the 1830s until it was wrecked in 1876.

# THE 19TH CENTURY

In 1840 transport to and from Bridgwater was by carriers' carts which ran daily from various public houses in Bridgwater. The Star was used for those wishing to travel to Huntspill. In 1841 Brunel's railway arrived in Highbridge and Bridgwater – there was a station at Highbridge, with a fine building, booking office, waiting room, etc., which was illegally demolished some years ago. The large buildings of the railway repair shops at Walrow also provided employment. The coming of the railway through the village in 1841 heralded the early demise of the stagecoaches which, over a period of some 60 years, had developed from the early Bristol-to-Exeter coach running three times a week in the late 1770s to at least eight stages, all with their own names, passing each weekday through the village in both directions. The advent of the railway was to put them all out of business.

Using local directories it is possible to develop a picture of just how busy the village was with stagecoaches and carrier wagons passing through – at a conservative estimate over 100 coaches and 50 wagons weekly! Amongst them were the *John O'Groats* and the *Self Defence* stages which both ran to and from Bridgwater to Bristol; the *Estafelle* running from Devonport to Birmingham; the *Economist* operating between Exeter and Bristol; the *Exquisite* between Exeter and Cheltenham and the *Nonpareil* which ran between Plymouth and Bristol, as well as the Bristol-to-Barnstaple mail coach. There was also the *North Devon* stage which ran between Exeter and London and, seemingly, if on time, came through the village during the night.

In 1823 Huntspill Court was put up for sale: the advertisement suggested that it was 'fit for the reception of a genteel family' but, more interestingly, it mentioned that 'a number of coaches pass the house daily, to every part of the kingdom'. The single fare at that time from Bristol to Bridgwater, or vice-versa, was 8 shillings sitting inside the coach, or 5 shillings braving the elements 'outside', which meant sitting on top of the coach. This was an improvement on the conditions endured by passengers in the late 1770s when everyone, inside or outside, was charged half a

## APPORTIONMENT of the RENT-CHARGE in lieu of TITHES in the Parish of Huntspill, in the County of Somerset.

Whereas an Agreement for the COMMUTATION of TITHES in the Parish of HUNTSPILL, in the County of Somerset, was, on the twenty-seventh day of March, in the year one thousand eight hundred and thirty-eight, confirmed by the Tithe Commissioners for England and Wales, of which Agreement, with the Schedule thereunto annexed, the following is a Copy :—

PROVISIONAL ARTICLES of Agreement for the Commutation of the Tithes, of the parish of Huntspill, in the County of Somerset, in pursuance of the Act for the Commutation of Tithes in England and Wales, made and executed at a meeting duly called and holden in the said parish, and adjourned from time to time, and now holden by adjournment on the fourteenth day of November, in the year of our Lord one thousand eight hundred and thirty-seven, and since perfected according to the provisions of the said Act, by and between the several Bodies Politic and Persons, owners of Land within the said Parish, by whom or by whose agents duly authorised in that behalf these presents are executed, and the interest of which Landowners in the Lands of the said Parish is not less than two-thirds of the Lands therein subject to tithes, of the one part, and the Reverend Noel Thomas Ellison, Clerk, Rector of the said Parish and owner of all the Tithes, as well great as small thereof, of the other part.

It is by these presents witnessed that it hath been and is mutually agreed upon by and between all the said parties to these presents in manner following, that is to say, that the annual sum of six hundred and ninety-one pounds, sixteen shillings, and fourpence, by way of rent-charge, (subject to variation as in the said act provided, and subject to the other provisions therein contained,) shall be payable and paid to the said Noel Thomas Ellison, as Rector of the said Parish and owner of the tithes thereof, and to his successors, instead of all the tithes, as well great as small, of the lands of the said Parish subject to tithes, (including the tithe of glebe, the rent-charge in lieu of which it is hereby agreed shall be fixed at the sum of seven pounds, ten shillings, in respect of all the tithes, as well great as small of all the glebe lands of the said Parish subject to tithes, and which item it is hereby agreed shall be apportioned exclusively upon the said glebe lands,) and instead of all Easter offerings, oxshoots, moduses, and compositions real and prescriptive, and customary payments payable in respect of all the lands of the said parish or the produce thereof, a summary description of which lands is contained in the schedule hereunto annexed.

And it is hereby agreed by and between the said parties to this agreement that the payment of the said rent-charge shall commence from the first day of April, one thousand eight hundred and thirty-eight.

In testimony whereof the said parties to these presents or their respective agents thereunto duly authorised in their names and on their behalf, have to these presents subscribed and set their respective hands and seals.

### SCHEDULE TO THE ABOVE ARTICLES OF AGREEMENT.

The whole parish of Huntspill aforesaid contains five thousand five hundred and ninety nine acres, one rood, and four perches of land, statute measure.

The whole quantity of the lands of the said parish which are subject to the payment of any kind of tithes, is four thousand five hundred and ninety five acres, three roods, and fourteen perches, statute measure.

The whole quantity of land subject to tithes, within the said Parish, which is cultivated as arable land is five hundred and twenty four acres, two roods, and twenty one perches, statute measure.

*Extracts from the 'Apportionment of the Rent-Charge in lieu of Tithes' for the Parish of Huntspill, 1838.*

guinea – quite a sum in those days. Some of the carriers' vehicles which passed through the village daily included Gane's wagon travelling from Bristol to Bridgwater; Bowering's wagon running from Bristol to Minehead, and Sealey's cart which ran from Burnham to Bridgwater. By and large, the carriers were not put out of business by the coming of the railway, and several of them ran on until after the first buses began to serve the village – National Bus service No. 1 ran between Taunton and Burnham and began in July 1920. One of the last horse-drawn wagons was operated by Hams of Berrow, who continued the service provided by Richards and Webb.

Just within living memory, the fare on a carrier's wagon, if space allowed, from Huntspill to Bridgwater and back, was one shilling; the wagon itself was strewn with parcels and packages and, if you lived on the main road and wanted any bulk goods transported, you left a large white card in your front window to alert the driver. These wagons crawled around Stretcholt and the back of Pawlett and took a long time to get into Bridgwater. An Act of Parliament passed in 1759 for the purpose of repairing several roads leading into the town of Bridgwater is interesting as it appears that by then the main Bridgwater-to-Bristol road came through the village rather than proceeding via the traditional, more hilly Glastonbury and Wells route. This latter route was known as the 'Upper way' and the Huntspill road was part of the 'Lower way'.

It seems likely that this was the Act that first established the Bridgwater Trust and empowered them to set up tolls and toll-gates on the roads locally. There were three toll-gates in Huntspill, although two of them – one named Newbridge (which was probably where the school is now), and one named Withy (by the Crossways) – were only operational for a few years. The main toll-gate, with house, was adjacent to the forecourt of what was Buncombe's Garage – just the Huntspill side of the Clyce. (The parish boundary in those days was the centre of the old bed of the River Brue.) The Bridgwater Turnpike Trust, which was responsible for the road system in and around the town, let these toll-gates by auction each year: the successful bidder had to pay the Trust a fixed rent but was able to keep what profit he was able to make. This main Huntspill toll-gate was opened on 11 December 1823 and the first tolls were raised five days later. In the early 1840s a William Snellgrove lived in the toll-house, which, unusually, was tithe free; i.e. no monies were paid for it to the Church. The Bridgwater Trust was abolished during the 1870s but the main road was still known as the 'Turnpike Road' right up until after the First World War.

All owners of land within the parish were obliged to perform six days' work annually on the highways and the turnpike (main road), and this to include one day's work 'composition making', which meant breaking up two tons of stone for use on the roads. A book listing all of these details still survives and on the inside front cover is the note 'implements belonging to the Highways, October 1815'. At this time these possessions amounted to 'one wheel barrow, a sledge hammer, a pick axe and a shovel'!

A letter written by the local author-cum-poet, James Jennings of Ilex House, to the *London Journal of Arts and Sciences* in November 1820, relates that John McAdam's supposedly new system of road-making had been practised here for the previous 30 years. Referring to the Cross-to-Bridgwater road, Jennings wrote: 'The part of the road to which I allude is that passing through Huntspill', and a local resident, Mr Thomas Greenwood, a Commissioner of the Turnpikes, was the person responsible for the system of laying small stones on top of slightly larger ones. Limestone was always used for any repairs. It must have been an enthralling sight to witness the stages, especially the mail coaches, passing through the village.

Brickworks were established at Highbridge and Bridgwater and a movement of people to Bridgwater can be detected from the Census Returns. The following, submitted by Mrs Greener of Huntspill Court, was published in the *Huntspill News* in 1976:

# A Royal Link with Old Huntspill Court

*It is a known fact that in many cases old houses have tales to tell, or they could recount romances, tragedies or circumstances of interest if walls could but speak. But as one can only sense the atmosphere of an old building occasionally, and then by a vague instinct, it is by more circumstantial and definite means that one may come by chance to hear of some event which is connected with an ancient building. What I am about to relate happened to us one day in the early nineteen thirties. My husband and I were going out one afternoon when we saw the figure of a woman walking slowly up the carriage-drive. She was short, seemingly of late middle age, somewhat solid and plump with a round face. On looking at her she immediately put me in mind of the late Queen Victoria: in fact her general appearance resembled that august sovereign to a remarkable degree. We stopped to enquire if there were anything we could do for her. She asked if she might be allowed to see Huntspill Court; she then opened her handbag and showed us an oval minia-ture on ivory of a young boy in a midshipman's naval uniform of the early-nineteenth century. The boy had a charming face, was fair with blue eyes and the miniature was beautifully painted. Our visitor told us that this was a portrait of her grandfather and that he was born at Huntspill Court, which was the reason she had travelled to Huntspill in the hope of seeing the house. His father was the Duke of Clarence, a son of King George III, who later became King William IV. The rest of the romance and family history was recounted to*

*Miss Young, who was living with us then and who showed her all the rooms in the house. They made friends and had a lot of chat over nursery tea. Here I may add that the acquaintance made that summer day developed into a lasting friendship, chiefly through letters as our unexpected visitor had come from a distance to see the birthplace of her forbear. The Duke of Clarence had met the lady of Huntspill Court at a ball in Bath and had sought further acquaintance by a visit to her home. This visit must presumably have occurred in the early 1820s. He became King William IV in 1830 on the death of his brother George IV, known for so many years as the Prince Regent. The Georgian royal Dukes had the reputation of being generous to their illegitimate children. This little boy was put into the Navy, was looked after and styled as a Fitz Clarence. I have always wished I could have talked longer with his descendant myself and have heard at first hand more of this romance of Regency days. I can see the little lady in my mind's eye still, holding the picture of a royal boy born at Huntspill Court, his granddaughter moreover looking like a reincarnation of Queen Victoria who was his first cousin and who ascended the throne of England in 1837 after the death of his father – who left no legitimate heir.*

# Local Directories

Directories from the 19th century can often provide clues about the people, activities and businesses which flourished locally. In the 1840 *General Directory for the County of Somerset* Highbridge is described as a small village in the parish of Huntspill where fairs were held on 11 August and 17 December. It is noted that in Huntspill, the Revd Thomas Howe in 1811 bequeathed a small sum for the education of poor children. The Tithes had been commuted for a rent charge of £684.6s.4d. Carriers' carts are described. For example, the 'Deacon's Cart' travelling daily from The Star public house in Bridgwater to Paulet Huntspill, Highbridge and Burnham.

The *Bristol Post Office Directory and Gazetteer* of 1859 includes mention of Huntspill's Post Office and Postmaster Mr Samuel Clouter associated with the same. There was a National School for boys and girls and the population stood at 1354. Red bricks, pantile, drainpipes and scouring bricks were being made at Highbridge. The railway had been built past Huntspill in 1842. Huntspill is again mentioned in a later *Post Office Directory* – as having a National School endowed to £6 and also a Sunday School. It is noted that the only trade being carried on was that of brick making in that part of the parish adjoining Highbridge (and the 1840 Tithe Map shows a brickyard near the Highbridge Hotel, on the Huntspill side of the old river). The Postmaster was still Samuel Clouter. Post was received from Bridgwater at 6a.m. and the last collection was 8p.m. The Burnett family

and Burnett's Stores are much in evidence: J. Burnett lived at Swell House and acted as Registrar of Births and Deaths, Assistant Overseer and had a 'Boarding and Day School', his father was at Ilex House, the Misses A. and E. Burnett had a 'Boarding School' also and Burnett Bros were implement engineers. In spite of the observation that there were no trades locally other than bricks, there was a remarkable list of tradesmen: E. Budge (plumber), Chas Churchill (saddler), S. Clouter (linen draper and PO), Thos Daw (shopkeeper), T. Palmer (miller), Batts Bow Steam Mill, Mrs Sarah Pople (shopkeeper), R.T. Palmer (miller and corn dealer), W. Haines (agricultural machine owner), W. Hardwidge (cattle drover), R. Mogg (cooper), Crispin Hodge (shoemaker), John Thyer (blacksmith), E. Toogood (auctioneer), W. Mitton (shoemaker), J. Lovelock (Crossways Inn and farmer), W.T. Martin (Globe Inn and wheelwright) and J.M. Poole (surgeon and coroner).

The 1883 *Kelly's Directory* records the population in 1881 to have been 1239. The Parish Clerk was Job Came and William Tilley was at Huntspill Court. In 1883 the land was 'mainly rich pasturage and applied to the manufacture of cheese of superior quality and other dairy products'. The School Board was formed on 11 May 1875 and a new school, near the church, was erected in 1876. John Rowe was Master and Mrs Anne Beacon was Assistant Mistress. The average attendance was 153. The Post Office was run by James Newton, who was also a draper and grocer. Letters arrived from Bridgwater at 6a.m. and 12.30p.m. They were dispatched at 12 noon and 8p.m. Other industries in evidence in the parish were listed according to name and occupation. Geo Clarke was a carpenter, Chas Deane was a shopkeeper, Charles Eveleigh was a boot and shoe manufacturer and beer retailer, Miss M. Ford ran a 'Ladies School' at Alstone Villa, James Burnett had a large store, Joe Budge was the blacksmith, Joseph Fackrell a beer retailer, Albert Holley a saddler and harness maker and Henry Squire a corn dealer. Isaac Stevens was a farmer and overseer. William Thyer was a hairdresser, Clement Toogood was the local veterinary surgeon and Jeremiah Wase was the surgeon for humans. The farmer at Porch House Farm was a person named Holley, an A. Pierce was listed at the Temperance Tavern. R. Sheppard was a coal merchant, Mrs S. Bishop was at the Crossways Inn, R. Toogood was the Registrar of Births and Deaths, S. Way was a market gardener, Charles Vickery was at the Globe Inn and also worked as a carpenter, and John Powell was a miller (water) and corn dealer at Huntspill Mill.

In *Kelly's Directory* of 1894 the following were listed: W. Brakes, farmer at Plymor Hill; Thomas A. Guy, Master Mariner; J. Hardacre, plumber; H. Squire, corn dealer; J.H. Sharp, surgeon; H. Lovelock, shop; Job Came, Parish Clerk and carrier; and 'Chief Landowner' Capt. Sir Alex Fuller-Ackland-Hood (Bart.).

*Looking towards the Globe Hotel, c.1910.*

West .. Huntspill

CORONATION 1953

E R
II

Souvenir Programme

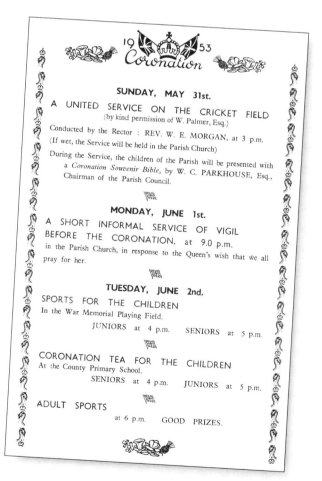

19 53
Coronation

**SUNDAY, MAY 31st.**

A UNITED SERVICE ON THE CRICKET FIELD
(by kind permission of W. Palmer, Esq.)

Conducted by the Rector : REV. W. E. MORGAN, at 3 p.m.
(If wet, the Service will be held in the Parish Church)

During the Service, the children of the Parish will be presented with a *Coronation Souvenir Bible*, by W. C. PARKHOUSE, Esq., Chairman of the Parish Council.

**MONDAY, JUNE 1st.**

A SHORT INFORMAL SERVICE OF VIGIL BEFORE THE CORONATION, at 9.0 p.m.
in the Parish Church, in response to the Queen's wish that we all pray for her.

**TUESDAY, JUNE 2nd.**

SPORTS FOR THE CHILDREN
In the War Memorial Playing Field.

JUNIORS at 4 p.m.    SENIORS at 5 p.m.

CORONATION TEA FOR THE CHILDREN
At the County Primary School.

SENIORS at 4 p.m.    JUNIORS at 5 p.m.

ADULT SPORTS

at 6 p.m.    GOOD PRIZES.

*Souvenir Programme of the coronation celebrations, 1953.*

*Advertisements from the* Parish Magazine, *1908.*

## *The Ilex Stores*

Above: *The Ilex Stores before 1910 with the ilex tree visible in the garden. The store dates from 1792.*

Left: *Sale notice for the Ilex Stores, 1909.*

Below: *The Ilex Stores during the 1920s.*

# THE 20TH CENTURY

Following the death of Queen Victoria in 1901 preparations for the coronation of Edward VII were made for 1902. A Coronation Festival Committee was set up with Dr J.H. Sharpe of Huntspill as Treasurer. A meeting of the Committee was held in July 1902 at the Board Schoolroom (Balliol Hall) which reported £20 in hand. Arrangements were to wait for the King's recovery from illness (appendicitis). The actual festival on 9 August 1902 was celebrated in grand style. The children were presented with medals from Mr H.W. Tilley. At 1.30 the procession, headed by the Weston Town Band, marched to the Parish Church. After the service they continued to the Chestnut Ground, lent by Mr H.W. Tilley. Some 800 sat down to tea in Mr Locke's marquee, including 500 adults and 300 children. There was a sporting programme, with the Revd Blathwayt acting as starter and G. Carew and G.F. Tilley as judges. In the evening there was dancing in the tent.

In 1904, Sir Alex Fuller-Ackland-Hood was still 'Chief Landowner' and two years later in 1906 Mr Newton was still at the Post Office, although mail boxes for collections had been placed at New Road and Withy Road. Burnett's Stores was still going.

*Kelly's Directory* of 1931 listed the following residents: William Greener at Huntspill Court, A.J. Amesbury at The Grange, L.A. Davey at The Elms, R.F. Clark was JP living at Greenwood and Sidney Phillips at Ilex House. Businesses included those of F. Cavill (nurseryman), J. Baker (blacksmith), F.J. Fowler (grocer), William Haggerty (fish merchant), William A. Sellick (cycle dealer), Walter J. Thyer (agricultural engineer), Chas Deane (shopkeeper), F. Jones (stationer and Post Office) and Stanley Washer (tea gardens). More recently there was Mr W. Parkhouse (also a grocer).

After the First World War there was a feeling within the village that there should be a War Memorial erected, as was the case in villages throughout the nation. A petition was drawn up and no doubt presented to the rector and ecclesiastical authorities. From its tone there would seem to have been some debate as to the memorial's location. The petition read as follows:

*We, The Parishioners of the Ecclesiastical Parish of Huntspill, hereby declare that it is our wish that the War Memorial Cross be placed in the churchyard of S. Peter's Church on the green by the Vestry Door on the North side, and in no other place whatsoever. In witness where of we, the undersigned Parishioners, have affixed to this document our several signatures. Dated, Huntspill, this 5th day of July, in the Year of Our Lord, one thousand nine hundred and twenty.*

The petition was signed by 159 parishioners. There is also a brass plate on the north wall of the church.

*The Post Office and Globe Hotel barn, late 1940s.*

Huntspill men found employment in the Brickworks at Highbridge and Puriton, the Saltworks at Puriton and in the Railway Carriage Works in Highbridge. Work was also available in Bridgwater at Morlands, Cellophane and the engineering factories, through all of which Huntspill people learned new skills.

Other 20th-century events of note include the outbreak of typhoid fever in 1938 which severely affected the parish. Much of the following is gleaned from the WI's history of Huntspill (1953). There was a sudden and serious outbreak in February of that year.

*The washing-up receipt for the Harvest Home, 1938.*

*A letter from the rector to the committee in thanks for a donation to the Huntspill Nursing Association following the Harvest Home, 1939.*

Influenza was rife at the time, and typhoid was not at first suspected. As soon as typhoid was identified, however, measures were taken to check its spread. The Isolation Hospital at Axbridge became the centre to treat the epidemic. The Rectory became the headquarters for consultation and for visiting all suspected cases and contacts. Two nurses from the Bristol Royal Infirmary lived there, visiting every house where a case was known or suspected – a procedure which, with the visiting of the rector and his wife, prevented panic and maintained morale. The rector started a press campaign, and a fund was opened which raised nearly £500, sent in from all over the country. A lady in Cheltenham sent a subscription because she had a grandfather clock made by a clock-maker of Huntspill. From this fund grants were made to families whose breadwinner was in hospital. Extra milk, eggs, groceries, etc. were provided for every house from which a patient had gone, so as to strengthen the rest of the family members against infection. The fund also provided extra coal and nourishment for returning patients. Coaches were hired to take relatives to Axbridge, where they were allowed to see their relation through the windows. When it was all over a special service was held, to include a welcome to returned patients, and this was attended by the Matron and several of the staff from the Isolation Hospital. The following news report appeared in *The Times* newspaper on 22 February 1938:

## TAUNTON, FEB. 21

*The outbreak of typhoid fever in Somerset would now appear to have spent its course. No fresh cases have been reported for the last nine days, and the authorities are of opinion that there is now no cause for undue alarm. Measures of control taken from the beginning have proved effectual, and the position is much better than it was a week ago. Moreover this assurance will be welcomed by seasonal visitors to the county – the outbreak has been confined entirely to the districts of Highbridge and West Huntspill, and the rest of Somerset, including the seaside and inland resorts, has been and is likely to remain unaffected. Altogether 39 cases have been reported and dealt with, 27 of which came from West Huntspill and the remainder from Highbridge. There have been six deaths, all of West Huntspill patients. The Axbridge Hospital of 40 beds has been reserved entirely for the reception of typhoid cases, the staff has been increased, and special consultants have been provided. The affected districts fall within the jurisdiction of two separate local authorities. Highbridge, a small township on the main Great Western Railway with a population of between 2,000 and 3,000, comes under the Burnham-on-Sea District Council and draws its water supply from the Axbridge and Cheddar reservoir at Axbridge.*

## Sewage Disposal Problem

*Huntspill is a straggling village a mile and a half on the Bridgwater side of Highbridge, and comes under the jurisdiction of the Bridgwater Rural District Council, which is also the water authority. No drinking water is drawn from wells or springs. The country is flat and marshy, and is intersected with reens which drain off sewage into the river Parrett, which later discharges it into the sea. The disposal of sewage has always been a difficult problem here, but a scheme has now been prepared at a cost of about £16,000 which is expected to overcome some of the difficulties. Although the county authorities are satisfied that these reens are not of primary importance in the present outbreak, they have undoubtedly made its control more difficult, and have now been cleaned out, limed, and generally disinfected. Immediately the first cases were reported, about the middle of January, Dr. J.F. Davidson, Medical Officer of Health for Somerset, with the cooperation of Dr. Norman Smith, of the Ministry of Health, and the officers of the local councils, set on foot an investigation, which included milk and water, as well as the dietary of the affected families. The latter was a particularly difficult piece of work, covering breakfast, dinner, tea, and supper, and included every member of each family.*

## Christmas Foodstuffs

*The investigation was extended to social gatherings and to various food producers and farms in the neighbourhood, and at length the evidence collected was sufficiently strong to point to certain foodstuffs eaten during Christmas as being the primary source of infection. This source is no longer operative, and there is reason to believe that the measures of control taken have had their effect. Precautions such as the boiling of all milk and water are still being observed, and the eating of ducks' eggs is officially forbidden because ducks frequent the reens, into which the typhoid bacillus may find its way. The state of alarm induced at first by the outbreak has now abated considerably, although it is stated that outside launderers are still chary of taking the washing of residents in the two affected areas. A relief fund has been opened, with the Rev. R.C.V. Hodge, Rector of Huntspill, as chairman, to assist the families of typhoid victims, most of whom are in poor circumstances. In addition to solid food, milk is 'provided for school children' who are unable to obtain it at the schools, as these are now closed. Grants are also made towards the funeral expenses incurred by families of those who have died from the disease, the provision of new bedding, and the fares of relatives visiting the patients at Axbridge. It is also hoped to be able to place the patients in convalescent homes for two or three weeks after leaving hospital. A sum of £350 has already been collected.*

The advent of the typhoid epidemic and the district's susceptibility to flooding apparently gave the Rector of Huntspill much food for thought. Likewise, a local news reporter seized the opportunity for some historical research and some supposition. The following article appeared in the *Bridgwater Mercury* on 15 May 1938:

## FLOODS AT HUNTSPILL
### *Fairly Frequent Occurrence*

*Present Rector's Reference: When preaching a few Sundays ago I quoted the old Huntspill motto: 'May the sea wall stand in front still And guard us all in Huntspill'. Afterwards I was told that our sea defences are no longer the secure bulwark that they ought to be. Can anyone who is in a position to know give a definite opinion on this matter? We have a right to know that our defences are in proper order and that the combination of high tide and westerly gale will not endanger out lands to-day as it has done in the past. We know that in the history of London the Great Plague was followed by the Great Fire. We don't wish some future historian of Huntspill to record that the plague of 1938 was followed by flood. Nor have I the least desire to emulate the exploits of the Old Testament Patriarch, Noah, and pay visits by ark to my semi-submerged neighbours.*

### *From Time of Romans*

*Thus writes the Rector of Huntspill (the Rev. R.C.V. Hodge) in the* Parish Magazine *for May. That in the past there has been good reason for the motto to which he refers is very evident from reference to the history of Huntspill. The district, as much as its seaside neighbour, Burnham, has undoubtedly been very much subject to inundation by wild seas in days that are gone so that there is every reason, even to-day, that sea defences at Huntspill should be maintained in as efficient a state as possible. At the same time be it remembered, the parish of Huntspill is geographically very much different from what it was in former times, and it is recorded that in the 18th century Stert Island was joined to the mainland. When reference to olden time flooding is made it is very probable that it largely applies to land which to-day is occupied by the estuary of the Parrett. One historian refers to Stert Island as 'a small part of the parish heretofore broken in upon by the sea, and now separated from it by the Parrett.' There is reference also to a sea wall reputed to have existed in the times of the Romans, and strength is lent to this belief because the sea wall would probably have been built to protect the Roman road which ran through Huntspill to Bridgwater. This mud wall, parts of which were visible up to recent years, if they do not still exist to-day, has long since been superseded by a stone wall evidently that to which the motto*

*Silver Street during the flood of 1981.*

*A group of villagers making their way through the flood water during the December 1981 flood.*

as far as Glastonbury. The sea, after its retirement, paid frequent visits to these parts, and it was found necessary to establish 'Commissioners of Sewers' who should examine the sea banks, sewers, etc. connected with the sea, and order the requisite cleansing and repairs.

# Houses Demolished

The first recorded flooding in Huntspill occurred after the date of the appointment of the first Commission (1304). One historian states: 'November 27th, 1703 – the sea broke into Huntspill about five or six o'clock in the morning, and broke down the sea wall and houses with a great wind.' A list of 17 houses thus demolished is given, and the inventory of destruction continues:

*Besides several hundreds of sheep and a great many bullocks, and all the wheat in the west side of the parish, besides a great deal of old wheat and hay that was lost in the waters before it went away.*

Apparently at that time a great storm raged all around Britain, and many ships and seamen were lost. In 1799 there was another visit by the sea which again broke down the sea wall, and the water remained for a considerable period. Happenings about this time bear out the suggestion that Huntspill today is geographically very much altered from what it was even a century ago.

*quoted by the Rev. R.C.V. Hodge refers. Exactly how long the present sea wall has existed is not known to the writer, but it is recorded in Collinson's* History of Somerset *that, 'at the extremity of the Stert Point, a long and narrow peninsula, the river Parrett emerges into the Channel'. The coast from this point north-wards is flat, and composed of vast sandbanks, repelling the inundations of the sea, which in ancient times, precedent to the birth of history, washed over these shoals, and flowed up into the country to a very considerable distance, covering with its waters that vast territory now called Brent Marsh, and the moors*

## Clyce or Clyse?

It is recorded that in the three or four years following the flood the 'Clyce' was made, the country being surveyed at the time to find the lowest level. Now there are two ways of spelling: 'clyce', the singular form, and 'clyse', the plural form, and they have vastly different meanings. The latter, 'clyse', means gates to keep out the sea, but whether these gates occupied the position of the present clyse at Highbridge, or whether they had a situation in the old river outlet is not altogether easy to tell. On the other hand, seeing that there is a reference to the lowest level – the reference might well be to 'clyce', implying the cutting of a new channel. This would well account for the two ways of spelling Clyse or Clyce Road at Highbridge. The road adjoins the clyce, the new channel cut for the river, while at the end of the road are the clyse, or sea gates. To which of these the roadway owes its name we will probably never know for sure. Records of further floods, taken from an old manuscript book written by the Revd F. Bennett (a one-time curate) of the history of Huntspill, are as follow:

*1845, January 29th – The sea flooded a great part of the road to Bridgwater, covered nearly all the West Huntspill field, and destroyed much wheat, vetches, and winter oats.*

*1849, October 26th – Great overflow of the sea, many hundreds of acres in West Huntspill flooded much damage.*

*1859, November – Sea overflowed; a great gap in the sea wall at Huntspill. The salt water covered several hundred acres of land.*

*1869, March – About 200 acres covered with salt water.*

*1870, October – From 200 to 300 acres covered with salt water.*

It will be noticed that in the more recent instances the area of flooding was greatly reduced, being only 'several hundred acres' in extent. Possibly this was due to a strengthening of sea defences, and the construction of the clyce – or should it be clyse?

## West Huntspill Welfare Clinic

Thanks to a number of kind villagers we have discovered that a clinic was held here as early as the 1930s. Babies from East and West Huntspill and Pawlett were brought to meetings, at first held at the Rectory then the Balliol Hall. The District Nurse for the area was paid for by the villagers, and the rectors' wives, Mrs Pizey and Mrs Hodge, organised these first meetings and fund-raising activities. In 1936 the nurse's bungalow was built in Church Road and she travelled many miles on a bicycle. A later mode of transport was the motorcar, as verified by photographic evidence. On inauguration of the National Health Service in 1948, the bungalow was purchased by the then nurse, Miss Dors. The District Nursing Service was incorporated into the NHS. A minute-book of 1950 costs the January party as follows: toys £4.18s.1d.; balloons 4s.0d.; cakes 17s.0d.; Christmas cake £1.1s.; bread 1s.10d.; tea 2s.9d. and sugar 5d.! A new minute-book had been purchased at 2s.5d. Food permits for the tea and sugar had to be obtained for the party. Members on the committee at that time were Mesdames Greener, Morgan, Haggett, Derham, Webb, Aish, Wynn and Brion. Whist drives seem to have been the most regular money-raising events. By 1956 the meetings were moved to the chapel schoolroom.

Pawlett became a separate clinic in 1962. In 1963 when there were 63 children on the register, the chapel schoolroom was considered to be overcrowded so again another move back to the Balliol Hall was considered. This took place in 1965. The last ladies to be involved with the clinic were Mrs Jean Davis and Mrs Betty Lambert who had served for a number of years as 'weigher' and Secretary. Mrs Barbara Bennett also helped. Miss Aish was our last visiting nurse. Lack of support led to the closure of the clinic in 1982 when there were only five children registered. It was at this time that doctors took on responsibility for the welfare of children.

After the Playgroup and Toddler Group moved to new premises on the school site in 1991, the health visitor paid regular monthly visits to the Toddler Group. This proved very popular as it was convenient for parents with older children at school and the mothers and babies enjoyed meeting friends and having a chat. This continued between 1993 and 1999 until, unfortunately, the service ceased when funds were no longer available. So many well-known people had helped over the years: Dr Burns and Nurses Dors, Moss, Gibbs, Waters, Clarke and Divisional Nursing Officer Miss Grace Webber. Among the many villagers who helped were Mesdames Solomon, Rouault, King, Hutton (Brewer), Burchell, Baker, Tippetts, Vowles, Bastin, Puddy, Bamber, Stangoni and Massingham. Please forgive us if we have missed anyone known to you. We are sure all the babies have been thankful for their care.

During the period of the Second World War most able-bodied men were away in the Armed Services or other allied occupations. The civilian populace endeavoured to 'do their bit' for the war effort as the following facts gleaned from the *Parish Magazine* testify. In December 1941 there was a collection of ship halfpennies for Missions to Seamen. Revd Hodge received 1660 coins weighing 21lbs, and the sum of £12.6s.0d. was sent to the Russian Red Cross. Jam was made by Huntspill ladies amounting

## Welfare Clinic

*Welfare Clinic in the Balliol Hall, 1973. Left to right, standing: Mrs Jones, Mrs Marsden, Mrs Doble, Mrs Phillips, Mrs Davis, Mrs King, Mrs Burchell, ?, Mrs Bennett, ?, Mrs Virgin, Mrs Deadman, Mrs Spooner, Mrs Lambert, Nurse Moss; sitting: Mrs Phillips, Mrs Ryden, Mrs Weeden, Mrs Jarvis, Mrs Martin, Mrs Brewer, Mrs Harvey, ?, Mrs Bamber, Mrs Burridge, Mrs Haines.*

*Welfare Clinic in the Balliol Hall, 1978. Left to right, standing: Mrs Davies, Mrs Davis, Mrs Orchard, Mrs Tiley, Mrs Stacey, ?, Mrs Holley, Miss Porter, Mrs Richardson, Mrs Little, Dr Little, Nurse Ash, Mrs Hawkins, Mrs Virgin, Mrs Smith, Mrs Lambert, Mrs Pengelly (senr); sitting: Miss Dors, ?, Mrs Ryan, Mrs Thomas, Mrs Greener, Mr Joyce, ?, Mrs Gardner, Mrs Mantell, Mrs Andrews, Mrs Pengelly.*

## Welfare Clinic

*Infant Welfare Centre (baby centre), Rectory lawns, late 1930s.*

*Nurse Dors outside her bungalow.*

*The Welfare Clinic at Huntspill Court, 9 June 1953. Miss Muriel Dors, centre, is in nurse's uniform.*

*The Garden Party for the Infant Welfare Clinic at Huntspill Court, 9 June 1953. The Mayor of Bridgwater, His Worship George Hayball, is cutting the cake. Mr W. Parkhouse is in the front row second from the right and Miss Dors is in the back row fourth from the right.*

to 672lbs. Two parishioners between them picked 1120lbs of blackberries! The *Parish Magazine* list of Huntspill parishioners serving in the Armed Forces who received Christmas gifts was as follows: W.P. Aish, N.S. Coombes, J. Coombes, S.C. Chedzoy, A. Dean, Gwenneth C. Foster, F. Foster, E.L. Foster, A.G. Fear, E. Garrat, H.A. Holley, L.R. Holley, W.A. Heal, B. Hooper, R.G. Hooper, H.R. Harding, W. Knights, F. Kingston, A.C. Kirby, C.H. Fackrell, W.J. Lawless, H. Marsh, J. May, J. Pidler, G. Peddy, B.R. Porter, H. Solomon, K. Violet Solomon, G. Short, R.L. Solomon, H.F. Solomon, E.G. Solomon, A.B. Short, R. Tippetts, E. Wratten, W. Walker, S.G. Woolley, J.B. Wade, A. Reynolds, S. Cavill, K. Peddle and Francis Hodge.

In January 1944 congratulations were offered to Captain F. Vere Hodge on receiving the Military Cross for 'gallantry, resource and devotion to duty', and also to Captain and Mrs Hodge on the birth of a son. In May 1945 Wilfred Hawkins became the first POW from Huntspill to return home.

The local Home Guard unit was a joint effort between Huntspill and Pawlett. The official title was 'Pawlett Platoon Polden Company 10th Battalion Somerset Home Guard'. Huntspill members included: Mr W. Parkhouse, who kept the Ilex Stores. As Lieutenant, was Mr Sheperd, who was the Bank Manager at Lloyds Bank in Highbridge but who lived in West Huntspill. Below is an extract from the *Huntspill News* of the 1970s submitted by Mrs Greener. It indicates that those in uniform weren't the only ones involved in the war effort.

## THE HOME FRONT

*I wondered if it would be of interest to read of the working party for the Somerset Comforts Fund which took place at Huntspill Court during the Second World War. We were registered as 'The West Huntspill Group of Workers – Som/W/72'. We met from May 30th 1940 to August 23rd 1945 and during that time we knitted 2,542 garments for the Forces and prisoners of war. These were taken to Bridgwater where I obtained the wool. I have three books of signatures and all the data relating to the meetings – we met every Thursday from 2.30–4 o'clock. The numbers varied from a dozen to thirty and the same people came regularly. We all knitted and we all had a cup of tea and a biscuit, ignoring the existence of rationing!*

My books register the number and description of garments knitted every month and also the weekly donation given by the knitters towards the wool. There was a balance at the last meeting after peace was proclaimed of £4.7s.5d. and the members agreed that this money should be given to the 'Welcome Home Fund', earmarked for the members of the services from Huntspill.

In the Bridgwater Mercury for June 1944 the following appeared under the title 'West Huntspill': 'Mrs. W.J. Greener's working party, which meets weekly at Huntspill Court, has just completed its fourth year, during which time over 1000 garments have been made for the Forces and prisoners of war. Mrs. Greener would like to take this opportunity of thanking all members, including those who attend weekly and those who knit at home, for their interest and support.'

The account given here of this war effort seems to be a list of statistics but that is just the summing up of the result that was obtained. The real meaning of the weekly event was the happy fellowship and enthusiasm for our chosen task we all enjoyed week after week. In spite of the joy and relief peace brought to everyone, at the last meeting members left with the feeling that something they had enjoyed together had come to an end. To me it has left many happy memories.

Parish Magazine adverts of West Huntspill businesses, 1940s.

*Local Home Guard and ARP. The men were mostly inhabitants of Pawlett and West Huntspill and are pictured at the Manor Hotel, Pawlett. Left to right, back row: Percy Smith, F. Wynn, E. Chidgey, Mr Riddell, W. Parkhouse, Eddy Parsons, William Powell, D. Difford, J. Poole, Mr Smith; 3rd row: Mr Claverly, G. Porter, Albert Hembury, E. Harwood, G. Reasons, V. Abery, Sid Mayled, L. Allen, Mr Cox, P. Stockham; 2nd row: Mrs Joan Long (KICK), Doris Staples, Mrs Buncombe, Mr C. Haggett, Mrs Buncombe, Fred Ash, Sgt W. Baker, Sgt Reg Sandy, H. Whitcombe, ?, Lt H. Sheperd, Sgt F. Hamlin, Sgt E. Nutt, Cpl W. Norman, L/Cpl B. Holley, Mr Cliff Wilkins, Mrs Gulliver, Mr Webb, Beryl Parsons, Mrs Lowdes, Mrs Webb; front: (Messengers and ARP) Sam Chilcott, Jim Edwards, ?, ?, Leslie Gulliver, ?, ?, Mrs Gulliver, Cecil Fry.*

*Letter received by Vincent Derham, then an 18-year-old man, from Mrs Churchill thanking him for his war effort.*

## Post-War Years

In the second half of the 20th century old houses such as Jennings Cottages south of Ilex House and the Huntspill Mill complex were demolished, as also were the range of barn and outbuildings at The Grange. New houses were built along Main Road, Church Road, Silver Street and New Road. New roads with housing have appeared: Alstone Gardens, Greenwood Close, Sunny Close, Plymor Road, Grove Road, Grange Road, Millgreen Close, Chapel Forge Close, Swell Close, Ilex Close and Sealey's Close. Off Sealey's Close Cara Mia Mobile Home Park has been expanded since its inception.

Huntspill suffered greatly from the volume of holiday traffic on the A38 until the opening of the M5 motorway in the early summer of 1973 which made it possible to cross the road again! Land to the east of the Ringstone Estate was purchased in the early 1990s by Sedgemoor District Council for use as a children's play area. It was passed to the Parish Council for purchase by a six-year mortgage. A managing trust was set up and the plot named Ilex Play Area.

In 1953 the village celebrated the coronation of Queen Elizabeth II with a programme of events over four days, from Sunday 31 May–Wednesday 3 June. There was a wide variety of events, ranging from open-air services, sports and teas, to dances and skittle competitions. The Parish Council presented a gift of a souvenir Bible to each child resident in the village.

In an edition of the *Huntspill News* in 1977, Mr Eric Solomon recounted his memories of the many and varied facilities that had been available within the village up to that time:

*Mr Sellick kept a cycle repair shop opposite the chapel, and in those days that was the place to go for valve-rubbers, bicycle spokes, carbide for cycle lamps, 'King of the Road', oil lamps or even inner tubes, and, with the advent of battery cycle lamps, spare bulbs and batteries too. He could even supply you with a brand-new bike if you wanted one, but sales were not too heavy as that would have set you back almost £4 in those days. Almost opposite the cycle shop was, and of course still is, the blacksmith's shop, owned in earlier days by Mr Jack Baker who, assisted by his son Ken, performed miracles of engineering amidst showers of sparks and clouds of steam, as he forged and fitted new tyres to cart and wagon wheels, or made and fitted new shoes to the ample supply of four-legged patients. In my schooldays it was a common sight every morning to see the considerable string of horses from Mr Ford Tilley's hunting stables at Alstone Court. They were cantered through the village by their grooms, the clatter of their hooves reaching into the classrooms like the sound of a cavalry regiment.*

## Post-War Years

*The Ilex Stores, c.1980.*

*Ilex Court (ex Ilex Stores), 1999.*

*The official handing over of the land for the Ilex
Play Area from Sedgemoor District Council to
West Huntspill Parish Council in the early 1990s.*
**Left to right:** *Vincent Derham, June Hooper,
SDC Chairman, David Tremlett, Jenefer Tiley,
West Huntspill PC Chairman and Neville Jones.*

*The demolition of
Huntspill Mill, 1963.*

*The Mill (now Millgreen Close).*

## Post-War Years

*Pageant performed for the Festival of Britain in 1951 on the Rectory lawn. John Holley is wearing the mortarboard and David Holley is supporting the slumped body. Marie Gannicot is at the back between them.*

*Ted Harding and Cliff Higgs at the Forge.*

## Post-War Years

*Meeting of the hunt outside the Crossways Inn, early-20th century.*

*Sellick's cycle repair shop, next to the Methodist Chapel.*

*Another well-known and respected member of the community for many years was Mr F. Fowler who lived at Ilex Stores with his wife and daughters Agatha and Mary. Both Mr and Mrs Fowler were staunch supporters of the Church, and his was a familiar figure in both East and West Huntspill as he delivered the weekly grocery orders astride his motorbike with side-car.*

*In those days Huntspill was well catered for in regard to shopping facilities. Starting at Pawlett Road we had greengroceries and fruit at Chedzoys of Bleak House (all home-grown stuff). Then came Granny Dean's shop at the end of Jennings Buildings which stood opposite the Crossways. (Incidentally, the last stand pump in the district stood on its pavement outside the shop.) In quick succession came Cavill's Nursery, the Cycle Shop, Mr Charlie Day's shop for decorating supplies, the blacksmith's, Huntspill Post Office, Walt Thyers for agricultural needs, Miss Nutt's grocery shop (now Sundowner) and for many years Mr V. Harris' sweet and tobacco shop at Laurel Bank. All of these in addition to a butcher and four pubs gave us a reasonable choice when it came to shopping.*

In 1975 the Wessex Water Authority was granted permission to build a sewage treatment plant near the sea wall west of Maundrils Farm. The proposed access was either through Alstone or Church Road using Leekbeds or Middlefield Droves. They rejected Alstone and chose the Church Road route. The Parish Council was concerned about this choice and a public meeting was held at the Balliol Hall on 11 August 1975, attended by 250 residents. The

developers noted the strong objections voiced. A Joint Committee of residents and officers of Wessex Water was established. The Committee consisted of: Mr Greener – Joint Chairman, Mr Skeet – Joint Chairman – Wessex Water, Mrs Hall, Mr Cavill, Mr House, Mr Downs, Mr Clark, Mr Ganfield, Mr Archibald – Messrs C.H. Dobbie & Partners, Mr Harries – Wessex Water, Mr Harrison – Wessex Water, and Mr Nesling – Wessex Water.

Four possible routes were then explored; the two previously mentioned plus access via Sloway Lane and a new road along the Huntspill River and sea wall or from Bleak Bridge to the proposed river/sea wall road. There was a further public meeting on 17 September 1975. The end result was a victory for the village with the Bleak Bridge route being chosen, although it was the most costly option. The following is quoted from the *Western Daily Press* of 18 September 1975:

*Villagers in West Huntspill, near Bridgwater, heard last night that they had won their battle to get Wessex Authority to change the proposed access route to sewage treatment works. But the change of route will cost an extra £70,000. The delay in starting the work on the new £1.5 million treatment works has cost an estimated £7,000 a month, giving a total added cost of £105,000. Villagers had objected to a route which would use Church Road because of a possible danger to life and property from a heavy increase in traffic. Following the public meeting attended by 250 villagers and water authority representatives last*

*Miss Nutt's shop, 1920s. The school is on the right.*

*month, a joint committee of residents and authority officers was set up and alternative routes discussed. Mr Lufkin Skeet, assistant secretary of the Wessex Water Authority, told last night's public meeting that it had been decided to proceed with the most popular of these routes. This would run from Bleak Bridge on the A38 and follow the Huntspill River. Planning permission had already been obtained for this new route and an agreement reached with the Nature Conservancy Council, which has an interest in the area. All this was achieved in less than four weeks. Mr Skeet told more than 80 villagers that the exercise had demonstrated how members of the public could get together with water authority officers to find a suitable solution. I would like to think that what we have done*

*here today will be repeated throughout the length and breadth of the land. 'We have learnt a lot,' he said. A decision on the route had to be made before October 1st when the date for accepting the tender ran out. The treatment works will eventually serve villages to the north of the Polden Hills and be connected to a main trunk sewer from Burnham-on-Sea.*

One of the notable events a year or two after this was the Queen's silver jubilee in 1977. As with the coronation in 1953, an extensive programme of events was organised. This included the distribution of 400 Jubilee Crown coins to villagers. The government of the day had declared an extra bank holiday to mark the occasion.

*Open-air Coronation Church and Bible presentation service at Grove Farm, 1953.*

*Balance sheet of the Silver Jubilee Committee, 1977.*

WEST HUNTSPILL SILVER JUBILEE COMMITTEE.

Balance Sheet 1977.

| Receipts. | £ | p | Payments. | £ | p |
|---|---|---|---|---|---|
| Football Club. Disco | 13 | 80 | Lottery Act. Registration | 1 | 25 |
| Mrs Sincock Raffle | 40 | 00 | Hire of rooms | 15 | 60 |
| Main Raffle. Nett | 84 | 00 | Lloyds Bank. 400 crowns | 100 | 00 |
| Donations | 7 | 00 | Service Sheets | 8 | 98 |
| Coffee Evening | 18 | 86 | St John Amb. Donation | 5 | 00 |
| House to House Collection | 154 | 92 | Insurance Premium | 12 | 50 |
| Profit from Donkey Derbt | 34 | 17 | Ilex Stores. Groceries | 31 | 39 |
| Donation from Cricket Club | 7 | 50 | Post Office do | 30 | 72 |
| Sale of Crowns | 8 | 50 | Childrens Teas | 81 | 08 |
| do of Goods | 25 | 51 | do Sports. Prizes | 15 | 00 |
| Sundry Receipts | 3 | 90 | Senior Citizens Teas | 31 | 50 |
| | | | Fancy Dress Prizes | 3 | 00 |
| | | | Jubilee Day Expenses | 30 | 45 |
| | | | Envelopes & Labels | 1 | 91 |
| | | | P.C.C. Duplicating | 3 | 40 |
| | | | Hire of Tent | 5 | 00 |
| | | | Balance at Bank | 0 | 51 |
| | | | Balance in hand | 20 | 87 |
| £398..16 | | | | £398..16 | |

proposed annual importation of cover material by sea would cause disturbances amongst the bird populations which frequent the part of the Nature Reserve adjoining the site throughout the long working life of the tip and that the intensity of the disturbances would increase with the westward progression of the tipping area towards the Reserve. The disturbances would also seriously detract from the value of much of the site as part of the area proposed for designation as a SSSI because it provides roosting and feeding grounds for birds from the Reserve. After the completion of tipping and restoration I would not expect the final land form to seriously affect the value of the site as part of a SSSI and I agree with the nature conservation assessor's view that it is likely that the quality of the NNR would recover.

Tipping on this exposed site would inevitably create a wind blown litter problem and attract large numbers of gulls and corvids which would be likely to disturb and harm birds in the adjoining NNR. These are serious disadvantages and I consider that they could only be avoided by continued, rigorous enforcement of a requirement that all tipping and initial covering operations must be carried out under a mobile net enclosure of the type proposed.

Although there is some difference of expert opinion on the precise agricultural classification of parts of the site it is apparent that the land quality on average is no higher than Grade 3C. The land is also subject to some inherent limitations which preclude any significant improvement and I do not consider it is of sufficiently high quality to justify a refusal on agricultural grounds alone. I accept that it may well prove difficult if not impossible to restore all the tipped area to its former land quality. Nevertheless I anticipate that some form of agricultural use would eventually prove practicable and that Alstone Court Farm would remain a viable, albeit smaller holding, during and after the tipping operations. The loss of the small area of Maundrils Farm required for the proposed access would cause some inconvenience because the land involved is mostly 'home' pasture, but it would not have more than a marginal effect on the viability of the holding.

Provided that the trial embankment now proposed on the northern boundary of the site is properly instrumented and constructed at least six months in advance of the construction of the main perimeter bund I am satisfied that the stability of the tip could be assured within satisfactory standards of safety.

With regard to the proposals for leachate containment and treatment I see no reason to doubt that they would prove satisfactory and that the site licence conditions agreed with the Wessex Water Authority would ensure that no pollution of the surrounding land or water courses would be likely to occur. On the other hand the hydrogeological assessor has advised that as an additional precaution a thickness of at least 4.0m of the Holocene deposits should be maintained below the floors of the tipping bays and I concur with this advice.

On the question of flooding I accept that the evidence indicates that it is unlikely to be a serious hazard. Nevertheless in such a low lying coastal area I take the view that there would be some risk of leachate and refuse escaping and causing pollution if serious flooding occurred after tipping had begun but before the site was entirely enclosed by a firmly consolidated bund of adequate height. This risk could be largely overcome by a condition requiring the completion of appropriate bunding before any tipping begins but it seems to me a matter for site licensing rather than planning control. Much of the proposed tipping area is sufficiently far away from the nearest residential areas to ensure that the on-site operations would not give rise to any serious offence or disturbance. It is apparent however that there would be occasions, sometimes of appreciable duration during the 30 year life of the tip, when the noises of operations such as bund building and tipping near the northern boundary would be clearly audible in the most southerly parts of Burnham.

If these occasions occurred during the holiday season I consider that noises from the site would be heard in a substantial part of the Holimarine village at levels likely to give rise to frequent complaints by holiday makers staying in the village. The occupants of some of the permanent residential properties in Alstone Lane would also be likely to suffer some disturbance by noise from refuse vehicles travelling to and from the site along the proposed access road.

In my opinion vehicles attracted to the tip would not give rise to any significant increase in traffic hazards whilst travelling along the A38 road. The proposal is however open to the objection that it involves the construction of a new access junction with a busy principal road and I consider it would generate conflicting movements at the junction at an intensity likely to cause some disruption of free and safe flows on the adjoining section of the main carriageway even though the proposed junction would be laid out in accordance with high design standards. I take the view that it would be preferable on traffic grounds to serve the site by an extension from the existing access road to the West Huntspill Sewage Treatment Works rather than create another junction with the A38. The disadvantage that increased use of this access would cause more disturbance to birds in the proposed SSSI and adjoining NNR could be largely overcome by a realignment of part of the road well to the east of the sea wall, but such a realignment would involve land which is neither included in the application site nor currently owned or controlled by the county council.

The visual and sometimes aural evidence of the presence of the proposed tip just across the River Brue from Burnham would probably deter some holiday makers who might otherwise stay in or visit the southern fringe of this popular coastal resort but I do not consider that the proposal would have more than a marginal impact on the holiday industry of the area as a whole. It is generally accepted that there is a need for further

Church Road during the flooding of 1982.

waste disposal facilities in Sedgemoor and I am not persuaded that it would be practicable or economic for the county council to meet this need by employing any method of disposal other than landfill at the present time. The main question relating to need is therefore whether it is of such urgency that it should override the planning objections to this proposal and rule out further consideration of possible alternative sites. In my view the evidence does not establish a degree of urgency sufficient to justify releasing this site for waste disposal on grounds of overriding need. Furthermore now that one of the key factors which determined the choice of this site for waste disposal in 1978 – the intention at that time to treat all leachate at a sewage treatment works – no longer applies I consider it reasonable to anticipate that an alternative site could be found where refuse tipping would give rise to a less significant combination of environmental, nature conservation and traffic objections than this proposal. A number of possible alternative locations have been suggested by some objectors but clearly much more detailed investigations and consultations would be necessary to establish preferability in all respects.

## The Compulsory Purchase Order

I have considered the county council's proposals and the objections relating to the Order both as made in writing and as presented orally at the Inquiry. The written objections were mainly on the grounds summarised in paragraph 5 of this report. There is no longer any need to include land forming part of the curtilage of 66 Main Road, West Huntspill, in the Order as the whole of this property is now owned by the county council.

With regard to the remainder of the Order land I am of the opinion that it would not be expedient to authorise the county council to acquire it firstly because the sole purpose for which it is required is to provide an access to a proposed waste disposal tip which I consider should not be allowed and secondly because use of the access would give rise to traffic and amenity objections which could be avoided by using an existing alternative route.

3.
The Inspector recommended that planning permission be refused and that the Compulsory Purchase Order be not confirmed.

4.
The Secretary of State agrees with the Inspector's conclusions and accepts his recommendations. Therefore he hereby refuses to grant planning permission or to confirm the Compulsory Purchase Order.

5.
The Secretary of State has considered the requests to reopen the inquiry following flooding of the site in December 1981 but in view of his acceptance of the Inspector's recommendations, does not consider this necessary.

The waste disposal site was finally established at Walpole in 1988. The house at 66 Main Road was still owned by Somerset County Council for many years after the compulsory purchase and the site located at Walpole!

## West Huntspill Parish Map, A Millennium Project

The first moves to establish a parish map were made in the spring of 1996 when some initial groundwork was done. Interest was re-fuelled in the summer of 1998 when regular monthly meetings of a working group, comprising the Clerk to the Parish Council, variously Eileen Shaw and Linda Dicker, and Parish Councillors Elspeth Allum, Colin Hall and Terry Orchard, began. It was decided to aim for completion as a millennium project. A public meeting was held in September 1998. With the aid of David Smith of the Community Council for Somerset, defined tasks were established, these being: a map to be erected on a cairn at the Common, a footpath guide to be produced, a history book of the village to be written and a time capsule to be buried. The working group from this point was aided by Charles and Madge Langdon. Research was undertaken and photographs were taken around the village of subjects that would be of interest. The services of Brian Wiles, a professional artist resident in the village, were obtained. Agreement to manufacture the finished panel was made with Arien Products of

Highbridge. To further involve the community a Parish History Exhibition was held at the school in February 1999. This was well attended and many people brought items of interest and a prototype of the map was displayed.

A survey of the parish's public footpaths was made. The paths were found to be in need of much remedial work. Therefore it was decided to postpone the footpath guide until the required work had been largely completed. The monthly meetings that followed the exhibition were mainly of an editorial nature, decisions being made regarding content and format of the map. An agreed map was finally established, the artwork completed and passed to Arien Products. The completed map was received in July 1999. Materials for construction of the cairn site were then sourced and costed. The funding for the parish map project had been from the Parish Council and it was agreed that additional grant fund aid be obtained. Various philanthropic bodies were approached and by late October 1999 the group were successful with funding, on a matched basis, with funds being given from the Somerset Community Chest. A site for the map on the Common was chosen and labour from the Bridgwater Training & Business Group arranged. Unfortunately design and weather problems on another of their sites prevented

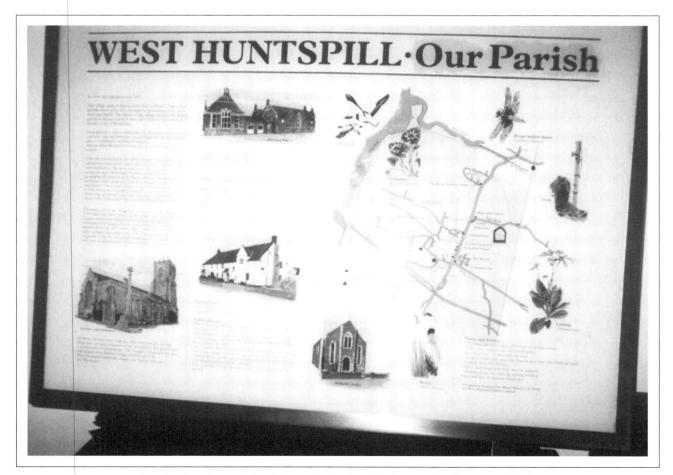

*The Millennium Parish Map, prior to installation on the Common, 2000.*

*The Millennium Project*

# PARISH MAP EXHIBITION

AN EXHIBITION FEATURING THE OUTLINE PLAN OF THE NEW PARISH MAP IS TO BE HELD ON
## SATURDAY
## 27 FEBRUARY 1999
AT WEST HUNTSPILL PRIMARY SCHOOL, NEW ROAD, FROM 2 PM

THERE WILL ALSO BE A SMALL DISPLAY ON THE HISTORY OF THE VILLAGE, TOGETHER WITH SOME VIDEO MATERIAL OF WEST HUNTSPILL PAST AND PRESENT

REFRESHMENTS WILL BE AVAILABLE

*Poster advertising the Parish Map Exhibition during preparatory stages of the project.*

## The Millennium Project

*Millennium Map cairn and seats on the Common, opening ceremony, 19 February 2000.*

*Parish Map and the project working group. Left to right: Elspeth Allum, Madge Langdon, Charles Langdon, Colin Hall, Terry Orchard, Eileen Shaw, Lin Dicker (partially hidden) and Brian Wiles.*

them commencing on the parish project until January 2000. Chris Drew and his team were extremely attentive to the village's requirements. The weather was the worst enemy of the project and Michael House of Plymor Hill Farm provided much-needed transport for heavy bulk items.

The autumn of 1999 was centred around designing a time capsule. Thanks to Terry Orchard and Mike Rees this was soon designed and manufactured. A wish list of items for inclusion in the capsule was drawn up and obtained from various parishioners. The capsule has been buried at the Parish Map site and it is hoped that the site, with its seating and paved area adjacent to the pond, provides a focal point of interest and a place for reflection for all parish residents and visitors.

The map was officially opened at 2.30p.m. on Saturday 19 February 2000 by District Councillor Mrs Jane Moreton. The map working group comprised: Chairman Colin Hall, Clerks to West Huntspill Parish Council Eileen Shaw and Linda Dicker, Elspeth Allum, Terry Orchard, and Charles and Madge Langdon. The designer and artist was Mr Brian Wiles, and the map was manufactured by Arien Products of Highbridge. The site was constructed by the Training & Business Group of Bridgwater, with funding being provided by West Huntspill Parish Council, along with a grant funding from Somerset Community Chest (represented by Rachel Ashman). Guidance came from David Smith of the Community Council for Somerset. The time capsule was manufactured and sealed by Terry Orchard and Mike Rees.

*The Parish Map, with seating area, pictured on the day of the opening, 19 February 2000.*

*Chapter Two*

# THE HUNTSPILL RIVER SCHEME

The object of the Huntspill River Scheme of 1939 was to drain the low-lying area on the south side of the River Brue between Gold Corner and Glastonbury, which formerly drained through the South Drain into the Brue near Bason Bridge. It was also designed to deal ultimately with the drainage of a similar area on the north side of the Brue which previously drained to the North Drain. After the Scheme was designed, it was extensively modified in order to serve an important secondary purpose, namely, the supply of water to the Royal Ordnance Factory at Puriton.

The Scheme can be briefly described as follows: water was lifted from the South Drain (widened for the purpose) by pumps at Gold Corner and made to flow along an entirely new channel, the Huntspill River, to discharge into the Parrett at Huntspill Sluice. The Huntspill River is 5½ miles long, with these leading dimensions:

|  | At Gold Corner | At Huntspill Sluice |
|---|---|---|
| Top width (ft) | 190 | 128 |
| Width of bed (ft) | 65 | 40 |
| Max. depth (ft) | 16 | 10 |
| Level of bed above O.D. (ft) | - 2.00 | + 4.00 |

*Aerial view over the River Parrett looking along the Huntspill River, 1960s.*

*Bleak Bridge, 1950.*

The side slopes were one vertical to four horizontal. The area of the water surface was 110 acres, and the volume of water in it 233 million gallons. At the time of the Scheme the river was crossed by five road bridges and one railway bridge.

Construction work was started in 1939 and finished in 1943. Up to seven dragline excavators were used, the largest of which weighed 43 tons and removed over a cubic yard of material at each bite. The quantity of earth excavated to form the new channel was two million cubic yards. The material was tipped on each side to form spoil banks, which were levelled and sown and now provide 250 acres of good grazing.

Gold Corner pumping station contains four 60-inch Sulzer screw pumps, each capable of lifting 275 tons of water a minute through a height of ten feet from the South Drain into the Huntspill River. Each pump is driven by a two-cylinder horizontal Crossley oil engine of 240bhp, running at 220rpm. Each flywheel weighs eight tons, and each engine uses about ten gallons of fuel per hour. The engines are started by compressed air, and the pumps are primed, or filled with water by exhausters which create a partial internal vacuum. The compressors and exhausters are driven by two 6hp oil engines, and there is a 15kw generating set driven by a 28hp oil engine for supplying electricity. There is a sluice valve in each pump delivery pipe, which can be operated by hand, by electricity or by compressed air.

Under the station there are four culverts, 12ft by 5ft, which allow water to flow by gravity when the levels are suitable. These are closed by penstooks which can be operated by hand or (in two cases) by electricity. The building is carried on 201 reinforced concrete piles, 50 feet long. It is 87ft by 48ft inside, and 24ft high, with a reinforced concrete roof, and it contains a ten-ton travelling crane.

Huntspill Sluice has two openings each 16ft and 8ft high. Each opening is provided with a tidal flap to keep salt water out of the river, a penning gate to hold water in it during the summer, and an emergency gate for use should either of the first two fail to close.

The following figures give an approximate idea of the costs of the major items involved in setting the Scheme in motion:

| Item | Cost |
|---|---|
| Gold Corner Pumping Station | £34 000 |
| Gold Corner Pumping Machinery | £25 000 |
| Railway Bridge | £37 500 |
| Huntspill Sluice | £34 000 |

The total cost of the entire scheme was about £420 000.

*Chapter Three*

# St Peter's & All Hallows

Before new churches were built at East Huntspill and Highbridge in the mid-19th century, Huntspill Church served a large parish extending over the moor towards Mark, Pawlett and Burnham-on-Sea.

The earliest part of the church still standing is the nave with its late-13th- or early-14th-century windows, large Ham-stone pillars (reddened by the fire of 1878) and string courses. No trace is visible of an earlier building, but documentary evidence exists of a church at least as far back as the 12th century.

In AD 1208 the 'Church and all its appurtenances' was donated by Fulke Paganel, the then lord of the manor to a priory which he had founded in Newport Pagnell in Buckinghamshire. A century later the church came back to the control of the Bishop of Wells.

A crypt existed and persons were buried there (under the south aisle) up until the 17th century. However, after the fire, the area must have been filled with rubble. The Cogan family were lords of the manor of Huntspill during the 14th and 15th centuries, a period of prosperity in the wool trade in Somerset. Contemporary tax returns reveal their wealth. They held various manors in the area including Huntspill and Alstone. The effigies in the niche on the south wall have been identified (*Somerset Archaeological Society's Proceedings*, Vol. 141) as probably those of Sir Richard Cogan and his wife Isabella, c.1386. An article on the tomb is reproduced overleaf. It is not thought the author of this report is correct in suggesting that this tomb is that of Sir Thomas de Cogan, for he died in 1315, which would

*Church kneelers.*

have been too early for this type of armour. The gauntlets shown were not introduced until about 1350. Sir William Cogan, who died in 1382, did indeed have a wife called Isabella Loring but she married again and so would probably not have been buried with him. The most likely candidate therefore is Sir Richard de Cogan, 1299–1363, and his wife, Mary Wigbere. It is not known whether the Sir John Cogan who died without issue in 1388 was married so we cannot rule him out entirely. But since the church was built about 1350 Sir Richard seems the most probable.

The Cogans were not always all they should have been; according to the Registers of Bishop Ralph of Wells, Thomas, a relative of the lord of the manor, was 'parson of the Church of Honespil' and he was accused of ejecting John Durbury from the custody of his own land of Baggedrippe, an action which he was brought to account for before the Justices at Westminster in 1353.

The south porch of the church, of later date than the nave, contains stone benches where parish meetings were once held. An upper window shows that there was once a room above, possibly used by visiting priests.

During the 15th century, when the area had recovered from the effects of the plague (the Black Death), the church was enlarged. The chancel was extended to the east and a Holy Water stoup is said to mark its previous extent. The Lady Chapel on the south side and the old Chapel of St Nicholas on the north side were also added at this juncture. The window on the north side of the chancel may have been blocked at this time, but there is some doubt about the date of the present rector's vestry; it appears to be of a later date than the Lady Chapel. The window may have been blocked at some later date when the north-eastern part of the building was added – a small window in the east wall is certainly more recent. On the wall in the choir vestry hang 18th- and 19th-century charity boards; records of gifts and legacies for the poor of the village.

Both the Lady Chapel and the Chapel of St Nicholas were robbed of their ornaments and abandoned at the time of the Reformation under Edward VI. Finally, the tower was added, or rebuilt. A stained-glass window at the east end of the church

# THE COGAN TOMB IN HUNTSPILL CHURCH
### (From *Somerset Archaeological Society's Proceedings*, Vol. 67)

*Person represented – Possibly Thomas, a member of the Cogan family, who were in possession of the Manor at this date, although the crest surmounting the tilting-helm does not appear to be the cognizance of this family. It may, however, have been a badge and not intended for a crest. Effigy – 6ft. in pointed basinet with camail attached, haubert 2ins. beneath cyclas, cyclas 16ins. longer behind than in front, baldrick 2 ⅝" adorned with rectangles containing four-leaf flowers, shoulder pieces, brassards, elbow-caps with small protecting plates, vambraces, thigh defences, ridged knee-caps with small lower plates, mail hose, rowel-spurs hands (gauntlets with gadlings) raised in prayer, damaged shield 1'7" x 1' on right arm, now lost all vestige of original colouring, guige (1 ¼") over right shoulder, sword (present length 1'10") with straight quillons and grip widening towards top, dagger on right side having scabbard (1'8") adorned with band of trefoil ornamentation with hilt (damaged) possessing quillons with twisted ends, Head on tilting-helm surmounted by mutilated crest of a human figure, feet on Lion (head lost) – Date circa 1345.*

*NOTES - The armour of this effigy is interesting because it represents the transitional stage between chain-mail and full-plate armour. This change took place in response to the increased penetrating power of the arrow and improved cutting power of the sword. At the contemporary Battle of Visby in Sweden knights clad only in helmet and chain-mail had both legs cut off and skulls cleft from crown to chin with a single sword-blow. The armour-plates over the chain-mail were designed to prevent such catastrophes! Since this description was written the lion's head has been replaced and one leg restored. \*\**

## Technical Terms:

*'basinet' (or bascinet) – a deep helmet covering the ears and protecting neck, worn alone with visor or with a great helm over it.*

*'camail' (usually aventail) – chain-mail attached to helmet and hanging down over shoulders.*

*'haubert' (or hauberk) – a coat of chain-mail.*

*'cyclas' – a tightly-fitting tunic more commonly worn by women until the 14th century when it came to be*

*worn also by knights over armour.*

*'baldrick' – a sword belt.*

*'brassards' – plates to protect arms.*

*'vambrace'– armour for the fore-arm.*

*'rowel-spurs' – spurs with little spiked wheels.*

*'gadlings' – spikes on the knuckle of a gauntlet.*

*'guige' – an extra strap for supporting a shield.*

*'quillons' – the cross-guard of a sword handle.*

*'trefoil' – three-lobed ornament like a clover leaf.*

*\*\* Incidentally it is probable that the sword was originally at least a foot longer than at present.*

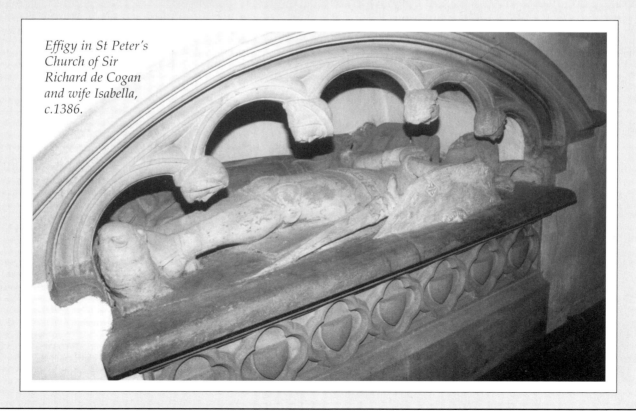

*Effigy in St Peter's Church of Sir Richard de Cogan and wife Isabella, c.1386.*

is a replacement for the one donated by the Revd Nöel Ellison which was destroyed in the fire of 1878. The present rector's vestry was walled off in October 1813 and a fireplace and chimney installed. It once had two floors and a 19th-century window at a second-floor level was added. The rood loft and the statues which once stood in the niches on the west face of the tower were also removed, but a door on the north wall near the organ opens on to a stairway to the roof and a blocked doorway above once gave access to the rood.

By the mid-l9th century, the interior of the church contained a gallery and ringing balcony under the tower and heavy wooden pews facing the pulpit; but all this was removed in an extensive repair and reno-vation of the interior in the spring of 1878. Then, sadly, in December of the same year, a fire was started by the overheating of a stove in the north aisle which destroyed the roof and the interior furnishings, leaving just the walls standing and the Ham-stone pillars reddened as we see them today. A report about the fire and the funeral bier written by an old parishioner Mr Solomon is reproduced on page 61.

Fortunately, the pulpit was saved with its fine Elizabethan/Jacobean carvings. This particular treasure has enjoyed a long and varied history having originally stood in Stogursey Church after which it was removed during restoration, sold to a church at Hotwells, Bristol, removed when this church was closed, then found in a shop at Bristol and bought for £10 by the Revd I. Gilbey Lonsdale in 1870! Along with the pulpit, part of the altar, the font cover, the painting of St Peter healing the Cripple and the 1660 Restoration Royal Coat of Arms were also rescued. The fire swept up the tower, bringing down and melting the bells and smashing the stone font. The stained-glass window at the east end of the sanctuary, given some years before by the Revd Nöel Ellison, was destroyed.

After great effort and the raising of £4000, the church was restored as nearly as possible to its previous condition, a new east window installed, and the building reopened within two years at a cost of approximately £3000. The stone corbels, half-length angel figures, each carrying a shield with one of the instruments of the Passion carved on it, were replaced, as were the stone heads in the nave. The choir stalls were carved by a local craftsman. One 'angel', found damaged in the churchyard, now sits in the south porch. The Lady Chapel was restored in 1947 and re-dedicated as a memorial to those who gave their lives for their country. In 1990 the area under the tower was refurbished as a choir vestry with a fine oak screen; a children's corner was provided and the font moved forward into the church. Since then removal of some of the front pews to the rear of the church has resulted in an open area in front of the pulpit.

The font in the church is modern but the 17th-century wooden font cover survives. Wooden frames contain a photostat of two pages of Martin Bucer's criticism of the first Prayer Book of Edward VI and the title page of the 'Huntspill Bible' of 1639/40, a black-letter Bible printed by Robert Becker, an early edition of the Authorised Version. This page reads:

*The Holy Bible*
*Containing the Old Testament and the New*
*Newly translated out of the original tongues and with the*
*former translations diligently compared and revised by*
*His Majesty's special commandment*
*Approved to be read in churches*
*LONDON printed by Robert Barber Printer to the*
*King's most excellent Majesty and*
*by the Assignees of JOHN BILL 1640*

Above the south door is the funeral hatchment of a lady, thought to be Frances Fane, daughter of William Rodney of Rodney Stoke, Somerset. Born in 1635, she married William Fane. The hatchment carries the arms of the Rodney family on the right and the Fane family on the left. A small oval brass in the sanctuary, rescued from the fire, records the death in 1687 of Elizabeth, a daughter of Dr William Fane by a previous marriage.

In the inventory of January 1948 the weather-cock is mentioned in the following terms:

*A very handsome bird of large size – all resplendent in gold – is ready to be erected on a flag pole on the Church tower as soon as this can be done. Dr and Mrs Wade are the kind givers of this most welcome and useful adornment to the church, and there are hopes that by the end of this month we shall be able to admire their gift in its proper place.*

It should be noted that not all who attended church were the models of good behaviour. The following three tales would seem to illustrate this:

## Huntspill Unworthy No. 1
### A Disturbance in the Church, 1649

Evidence was given to Sir Thomas Wroth on 17 August 1649, that Christopher Theare came into the church at Huntspill and sat near the pulpit with his hat on his head. When Mr Walrond asked him if that was a reverend gesture to be used in the house of God in the ordinance of prayer, he replied that he knew not that prayer was an ordinance of God, nor that the church was any more the house of God than any other common house, and so continued with his hat on till the sermon was ended. Then he began to argue with Mr Savage, the minister, about the meaning of a text quoted in his sermon. Upon being rebuked a second time and told that his carriage in the time of preaching and praying was not allowed by the Parliament, he replied that he did not reckon of the Parliament or of the ordinances and went as far as to say that the ministry of England were the ministers of the Pope.

## St Peter's

*North-east view of Huntspill Church, 1843, by John Buckler.* (Pigott Collection)

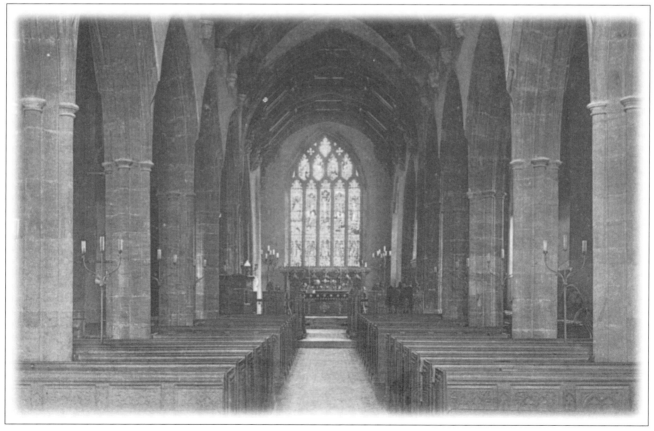

*The church interior.*

## St Peter's

*The church from the south-west
(without a bell-tower door), 1843.*

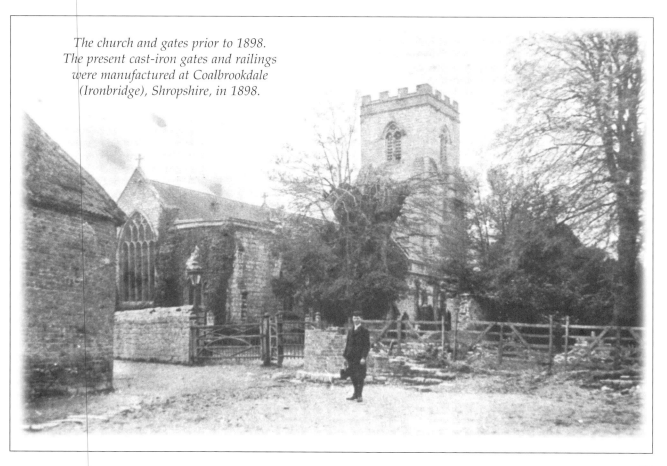

*The church and gates prior to 1898.
The present cast-iron gates and railings
were manufactured at Coalbrookdale
(Ironbridge), Shropshire, in 1898.*

## St Peter's

*The Rectory, c.1910.*

*The church gates and Rectory, c.1910.*

## Huntspill Unworthy No. 2
### An outspoken critic of the Bible and Parson

A few years after Christopher Theare had been reported to the magistrates for insisting on wearing his hat in church, a yet more unorthodox Christian appeared in the person of one William Allan of Huntspill. In 1656 it was reported by Thomas Bennett of Huntspill that William had declared that 'the Holy Scriptures were but as fables or a ballatt (ballad)', that there was no necessity for prayer or any other godly exercise to be used, that a man should be left to live as profanely as he wished, and that he should be saved if he thought himself to be in Christ! It's surprising how far back 'modern' disillusion with the Bible seems to go! The last remarks, however, are not heard often today. They sprang from an extreme form of Calvinism which took the view that if God had chosen you to be saved you could be as wicked as you liked without it making any difference; a comforting thought no doubt, but not one approved of by either Church or State!

It goes without saying that William duly appeared before the magistrates. Any reprimand or punishment he received, however, seems to have left him completely unabashed, for in 1657 he is found appearing before them again for having said of the then rector 'he doth preach lyes from ye pulpit'. So readers can see that in the 'good old days' of Cromwellian Huntspill, the unhappy parson's lot was no easier than it is today!

## 'Excuse Me That's My Pew!'
### Letter to Mr J. Cripps and Mr H. Jeffery
### (churchwardens), Huntspill

*Whereas information and complaint have been laid before me that Mr. Charles Hawkins of the parish aforesaid, who is himself in possession of an ancient and accustomed seat in the same, has of late more than once lowered himself into the pew of Mr. William Saunders legally, for a long period of time occupying the same with his family. I therefore the Ordinary of the said Church do hereby authorize and require you in case the said Mr. Hawkins should again so offend, to put the law in force against him and to use all legal Means for his being punished accordingly.*

Gee. H. (Bath & Wells)
20th. Sept. 1833

*Note: Rented pews disappeared from most churches long ago, but especially in the 18th and 19th centuries, when collections were very much less frequent than they are today, pew rents were a favourite device for raising Church funds. Visitors to East Huntspill Church can still see the box pews, formerly rented, in the front, and the benches for the poor at the back. Strangely enough it is the latter which seem the most popular nowadays!*

## AN UNCOMMONLY EPISCOPAL CHAIR

*(by Joyce W.G. Greener, Huntspill News, 1970s)*

*In the sanctuary of St. Peter & All Hallows Church, Huntspill, there stands an oak chair of the early-Victorian period... In the middle years of the 19th century it was owned by my Grandfather and stood in the hall of his house in the village of Hatherleigh in Devon. When a Confirmation was to be held in the Church and to be taken by the then Bishop of Exeter, Dr. Frederick Temple, it was lent to the Church... at which my father as a young boy was confirmed. It was then returned to the family home. Bishop Temple was later translated from Exeter to be 'Bishop of London', and as a very old man he became Archbishop of Canterbury.*

*He was just able to crown King Edward VII in 1902 but died very shortly after. At the Coronation service he stumbled, and the Sovereign leaned from where he sat on the famous chair in Westminster Abbey to support the old Archbishop. The present Bishop of Malmesbury is a great-grandson of Archbishop Temple (whose son William also became Archbishop of Canterbury) and at a service, recently given by the St. John's Ambulance Brigade of the County of Avon in Bristol Cathedral, Bishop Temple preached. I asked Mrs Temple if the incident my father had told me about was true as I had never heard it except as a child from him. 'Yes', she said it had occurred. The Archbishop was old and was weighed down by his episcopal cape, etc. So that he had remained in my father's remembrance since he was a child, and in mine too. The oak chair in after years came to me. Once more at a Confirmation, this time in Huntspill Church, nearly a hundred years later, there was no suitable chair for the Bishop to sit in. The Revd R.C.V. Hodge kindly used it on that occasion, and later, with the consent of the P.C.C., accepted it and obtained a faculty for it to remain permanently in the church.*

*The chair has been honoured in use by a Bishop of Exeter, a Bishop of London, an Archbishop of Canterbury and lastly by one of our own Bishops of Bath and Wells.*

*The other two chairs in the chancel were bought by the late Revd C.E. Pizey and presented to the church.*

## St. Peter's Church, Huntspill.

CLERGY :
Rector—Rev CHARLES REGINALD BLATHWAYT.
Curate—Rev. FREDERICK J. H. AXFORD.

CHURCHWARDENS :
Mr. GILBERT J. BURNETT AND Mr. EDWIN VOWLES.

SIDESMEN :
Mr. EDWIN BOWRING,          Mr. FREDERIC HOUSE,
Mr. W. W. HOUSE,            Mr. N. J. REYNOLDS.

DISTRICT VISITORS :
Mrs. IRELAND,               Miss A. BURNETT,
Mrs. BOWRING.               Mrs. ROGERS,
Miss SCARLE,                Mrs. PITTS,
Mrs. SPICKETT,              Miss BESSIE STEVENS,
Mrs. GILBERT BURNETT.       Miss FLORA CHICK.

ORGANIST :
Mr. HARRY BASTARD.

DEPUTY CLERK & SEXTON :
Mr. WILLIAM SELLICK.
Mr. SELLICK should be informed of Baptisms or Burials

CHURCH SERVICES :
On Sunday at 11 a.m. and 6.30 p.m. ; Celebration of Holy Communion on the first and third Sunday in the month at mid-day ; other Sundays at 8.30 a.m.

Children's Service and the Sacrament of Holy Baptism first Sunday in the month at 3 p.m. Daily Matins at 8.30 a.m.

*The Church is always open.* Will you sometimes make use of its hallowed silence for prayer for yourself and the parish, even if you are unable to come to the daily service ?

Parishioners, who at any time wish to see either of the clergy, are requested to send a note either to Rev. C. R. BLATHWAYT or Rev. F. J. H. AXFORD, and they will receive an immediate visit.

*St Peter's Church, clergy and officers, 1908.*

## Saint Peter's Church, Huntspill.

CLERGY :
Rector—Rev. CHARLES EDWARD PIZEY.

CHURCHWARDENS :
Mr. EDWIN VOWLES and Mr. FREDERICK HOUSE.

SIDESMEN :
Mr. E. BOWRING,             Mr. C. HANCOCK,
Mr. F. ILEY,                Mr. W. W. HOUSE,
Mr. J. RABBITT,             Mr. N. J. REYNOLDS,
Mr. H. E. VOWLES,           Mr. J. BAKER,
Mr. H. RABBITT,             Mr. J. KIMBER,
Mr. H. P. BURNETT,

DISTRICT VISITORS :
Mrs. BICKNELL,              Miss D. HOUSE,
Mrs. BOWRING,               Mrs. PIZEY,
Miss MATTHEWS,              Mrs. ROGERS,
Miss FLORA CHICK,           Miss SCARLE,
Mrs. HOOPER,                Mrs. SPICKETT,

ORGANIST :
Mr. HARRY BASTARD.

DEPUTY CLERK AND SEXTON :
Mr. WILLIAM SELLICK.
Mr. Sellick should be informed of Baptisms or Burials.

CHURCH SERVICES :
On Sunday at 11 a.m. and 6.30 p.m. ; Celebration of Holy Communion on the First and Third Sundays in the Month at mid-day ; other Sundays at 8.30 a.m.

Children's Service and the Sacrament of Holy Baptism First Sunday in the Month at 3 p.m. Daily Matins at 8.30 a.m. Celebration of Holy Communion on all Saints' Days at 8.30.

*The Church is always open.* Will you sometimes make use of its hallowed silence for prayer for yourself and the parish, even if you are unable to come to the daily service ?

Parishioners, who at any time wish to see the clergy, are requested to send a note to the Rectory and they will receive an immediate visit.

*St Peter's Church, clergy and officers, 1912.*

## St. Peter's Church, Huntspill.

PAROCHIAL CHURCH COUNCIL.
Chairman : Rev. Charles E. Pizey.      Vice-Chairman : Mr. H. Brown.
Churchwardens : Mr. C. Hancock and Mr. G. V. Sheppard.
Members : Miss Chick, Mr. Fowler, Mr. Kimber, Mr. Mason, Mr. W Parkhouse,
Mrs. Pizey, Mr. H. Slocombe, Mrs. Sheppard, Mr Sellick,
Mr. W. S. Tilley, Mr. Washer.

Hon. Secretary : Mr. L. A. Davey.

SIDESMEN.
Messrs. J. Brown, J. Kimber, W. Parkhouse, W. Sellick, A. Slocombe,
Leslie Toogood and S. Washer.

DISTRICT VISITORS.
Mrs. Davey, Miss House, Miss Haines, Miss Needs, Mrs. Pizey, Miss Pizey,
Mrs. Reynolds, Miss D. Tilley, Miss Thomas and Miss Watts.

CHURCH SERVICES.
On Sundays at 11 a.m. and 6.30 p.m. Celebration of Holy Communion on the First and Third Sundays in the Month at mid-day ; other Sundays at 8.30 a.m.

Children's Service and the Sacrament of Holy Baptism First Sunday in the Month at 3 p.m. Daily Matins at 8.30 a.m. Celebration of Holy Communion on all Saints' Days at 8.30 or 10 o'clock.

*The Church is always Open.* Will you sometimes make use of its hallowed silence for prayer for yourself and the parish, even if you are unable to come to the daily service ?

Parishioners who at any time wish to see the Rector are requested to send a note to the Rectory, and they will receive an immediate visit.

*St Peter's Church, Parochial
Church Council and officers, 1924.*

## St. Peter's Church, Huntspill.

PAROCHIAL CHURCH COUNCIL.
                                        Vice-Chairman : Mr. W Parkhouse.
Chairman : Rev. Charles E. Pizey.
Churchwardens : Mr. C. Hancock and Mr. G. V. Sheppard
Members : Mr. W. Sellick, Mr. J. Kimber, Mr. Yorke, Mr. F. Jones,
Mr. O. Perham, Mr. P. Hansford, Mrs. Pizey, Mrs. Reynolds,
Mr. E. Watts, Mr. A. Braund, Mrs. Yorke, Mrs. Watts, Miss Chick,
Mrs. Sheppard, Mrs. Yorke, Miss Needs, Miss C. Needs.
Hon. Secretary : Mr. L. A. Davey.

SIDESMEN.
— Messrs. Yorke, J. Kimber W. Parkhouse, W. Sellick, E. Watts,
O. Perham and A. Braund
ORGANIST : Mrs. Pizey.      DEPUTY ORGANIST : Mr. L. A. Davey.

CHOIRMEN.
Messrs. Hancock, Hansford, Mason, Adams (Tenors), W. Needs (Alto),
Washer, Braund, Wide, Slocombe, T. Hunt (Basses).

CHOIRBOYS.
E. Reynolds, A. Deane, A. Hobbs, R. Harding, W. Perry, D. Steele, J. Davis,
G. Woolley, G. Short, H. Harding, E. Young, A. Solomon,
J. Hobbs and F. Haggett.

SUNDAY SCHOOL TEACHERS.
Mrs. Pizey, Miss Pizey, Miss Needs, Miss D. Bevan, Miss E. Derham,
Mrs. G. Neath, Miss B. Turner and Nurse Coombes.

DISTRICT VISITORS.
Mrs. Davey, Miss House, Miss Haines, Miss Needs, Miss Pizey, Mrs. Reynolds,
Miss D. Tilley, Miss Thomas, Miss Watts, Miss M. Fear and Miss M Watts.

BELL-RINGERS.
Messrs. T. Davey, C. Hancock, W. Hooper, W. Parkhouse, H. Parkhouse,
O. Perham, W. G. Sellick, A. Turner, A. Randall.

Presiding Associates for M.U.—Mrs. Pizey and Mrs Burnett.
                          G.F.S.—Mrs. Pizey and Mrs. Baker.

CHURCH SERVICES.
On Sundays at 11 a.m. and 6.30 p.m. Celebration of Holy Communion on the First and Third Sundays in the Month at mid-day ; other Sundays at 8.30 a.m.

Children's Service and the Sacrament of Holy Baptism First Sunday in the Month at 3 p.m. Daily Matins at 8.30 a.m. Celebration of Holy Communion on all Saints' Days at 8.30 or 10 o'clock.

*St Peter's Church, Parochial
Church Council and officers, 1928.*

# RESTORATION OF THE PARISH CHURCH
(Bridgwater Mercury, *21 April 1878*)

*During the past seven or eight months the Parish Church of Huntspill, dedicated to St. Peter, has been undergoing partial restoration at a cost of something like £1,200 by Mr Thomas Searle, builder, of Bridgwater, from the designs and under the superintendence of Messrs Hans, Price and Wooler, of Weston-super-Mare; and the work being now completed, the sacred edifice was formally reopened on Easter Tuesday. The services have lately been held at the newly erected Board Schools. These were built by Messrs Chedzoy and Son, of Bridgwater, in accordance with plans furnished by Messrs Down and Son, of the same place, for the sum of £350 and capable of accommodating 240 children.*

*St. Peter's church is a good example of late Perpendicular work. The roofs of the Nave and Aisles being in a very decayed state it was decided last year to have them thoroughly repaired. The Chancel roof was repaired some thirty years ago and the Church, since that time, has been re-seated; but the lead in the roofs of the nave and aisles was in a very bad state, and the timber in some places much decayed. In the nave was a heavy plaster ceiling hiding the whole of the woodwork. As the funds available were insufficient for the restoration of the lead roof it was determined to sell the old lead and cover the nave roof with Staffordshire tiles, as had already been done in the case of the chancel roof. The aisle roofs, which were too flat for these tiles, have been covered with French tiles, made of stout zinc with felt between the board and tiles. The old panelling of aisle roofs has been restored and new panelling introduced in the chancel aisles, where the original roof had disappeared. The nave roof has been restored to its original form – that of an arched plaster ceiling, with wooden moulded vaulting ribs and barred bosses at the intersections. A moulded and battlemented cornice has been added; and an oak cornice of a similar description has been fixed in the aisles. A new panelled ceiling has been placed in the vestry in the place of the old dilapidated plastered ceiling. The whole of the exposed timber has been stained a dark oak colour. The ringing floor and unsightly gallery at the west end have been removed and the tower thrown open to the church; and the large west window has been filled with new tracery in Ham Hill stone, and glazed with cathedral glass. A new approach has been made to the ringing floor and the peal of bells has been remodelled by Messrs Taylor of Loughborough, and re-hung and they are now rung from the upper floor of the tower. The font has been removed from the north aisle and placed on a new Ham stone base in the Tower. The old heating apparatus has been removed and new stoves have been fixed. Stacks of pipes have also been provided to carry off the water to the new drains in place of the spout, the effect of which will be to keep the churchyard drier.*

*The whole of the work is generally acknowledged to have been executed in a highly satisfactory manner. Some extra work has been done at the private expense of the highly esteemed Pastor (Rev. J.A. Lonsdale).*

# FROM MR SOLOMON'S NOTES

*During the fire the bells melted and the metal fell through to the floor below. The bells were made by John Taylor, Loughborough, and were of a particularly 'pure' metal, which accounts for the fine tone. The metal was saved for re-casting – only 6 bells this time as there were not enough left overs. The fire was caused by the overheating of the 'tortoise' stove in the church.*

*The discovery of the church fire was made by my grandfather Mr Frank Day. He was the local butcher and lived in the second cottage in Cadwells Lane. On the night of the fire, he was walking through the churchyard at 11.45p.m. having visited a friend in Saloway Lane. He went to the Rectory to arouse the Rector, the Rev Wilson, and in so doing, disturbed the dog. This was in the year 1878 when my grandfather was 32 years of age.*

*Sometime in the early part of the last century, the date escapes me, but can be checked on the right hand charity board in the NW alcove of the church, a sum of £200 was left in trust, the interest was to be spent on blankets for the poor and needy. I remember as a boy about 20 to 25 blankets were given out each year; I believe now the amount of interest is in little excess of the cost of 1 blanket and I believe the scheme has been dropped.*

*In passing, a former Rector of West Huntspill, the Rev John Tripp was the great, great, great, great, great grandfather of Capt Mark Phillips. This was confirmed by* The Times *and I gave the confirmation to the Rev Hodge.*

*West Huntspill is one of the few remaining villages in Somerset to still possess the funeral bier. If it can still be called a possession. I last remember it being used in 1938 to convey the corpse of Mr William Rufus King to the churchyard. It can be found in the old shed attached to the Balliol Hall – but what a sad sight it is.*

*Incidentally it was my Uncle Reg's job to keep it clean and polished, when he was head coachman to the Rev Blaithwaite.*

## Events

*The Sunday School outing to Sidmouth, late 1950s.*

*St Peter's Harvest Supper Committee's entry for East Huntspill's Harvest Home procession in the 1970s.* Standing on float, *left to right:* Michael Watts, John Davey, Lloyd Burchell, Judith Virgin; front: *Ted Lambert, Baden Cann, Fred House, David Holley, Fred Psyk.*

*Church Fête at Grove Farm.*

## Events

*St Peter's Garden Fête, mid 1950s. Pam and Barbara Haggett are entered
in the fancy-dress competition and Pam is dressed as 'Departed Spirits'.*

## Events

*Easter church procession led by the Verger, Herbie Hawkins, c.late 1970s.*

*Dedication of the churchyard extension, 12 December 1990. The Revd Jim Hill is centre and Charles Langdon is on the right.*

# CLERGY OF HUNTSPILL

| DATES | INCUMBENT | CAUSE OF VACANCY |
|---|---|---|
| By 1280–95+ | Gilbert de Woolavington | |
| By 1315–44 | John de Cogan | |
| 1344–52+ | Thomas de Cogan | |
| By 1359–68 | Walter de Aldebury, Prebendary of Wells and London | |
| 1368–78 | John de Northwode | Exchange |
| 1378–85 | Robert Dedwith | |
| 1385–1415 | William Loryng DCL, Canon of Lincoln, Salisbury & Bangor, Constable of Bordeaux | |
| 1415–53 | John Arundel MA, Dean of St George's, Canon & Prebendary of Wilton, Auckland & Wells, Master of St Bartholomew's Bristol | Death |
| 1453–57 | Nicholas Carent, Dean of Wells | Death |
| 1468–95 | John Bourgchier, Archdeacon of Buckingham & Canterbury, Prebendary of Wells | |
| 1496–1524 | Thomas Bourgchier MA | Death |
| 1524–33 | John Togood | Death |
| 1533–57 | Walter Cretyng DCL, Archdeacon of Bath | Death |
| 1557–58 | John Smith BA, Rector of North Petherton | Death |
| 1558–78 | Thomas Jennings | Death |
| 1578–1617 | John Parsons MA, BD, BCL, Prebendary of Wells | Death |
| 1617–26 | Oliver Ormerod MA | Death |
| 1626–46? | John Hayne MA | |
| By 1649– | Mr Savage (intruded) | |
| 1650–79 | William Fane STP, Prebendary of Wells | |
| 1679–1708 | Samuel Woodesaon BA | Death |
| 1708–39 | John Tripp MA | Death |
| 1739–67 | Joseph Sandford MA | Death |
| 1767–78 | Theophilus Leigh DD, Master of Balliol | Resignation |
| 1778–1804 | George White MA | |
| 1804–19 | Thomas Howe MA | Death |
| 1819–23 | Thomas Cook Rogers MA | Death |
| 1823–58 | Nöel Thomas Ellison MA | |
| 1858–70 | William Charles Lake MA, afterwards Dean of Durham | Death |
| 1870–73 | Henry Wall MA, Professor of Logic, Oxford | Resignation |
| 1873–78 | James Gilby Lonsdale MA | Death |
| 1878–94 | William Osborne Pocock Wilson MA | Resignation |
| 1894–1912 | Charles Reginald Blathwaite MA | Exchange |
| 1912–32 | Charles Edward Pizey MA | Death |
| 1932–46 | Roger Cuthbert Vere Hodge MA | Death |
| 1946–55 | William Edgar Morgan, Prebendary of Wells | Cession |
| 1955–70 | John Stewart MacArthur DD | |
| 1971–82 | Alun John Morris Virgin MA | Resignation |
| 1976 | Rector of United Benefice of Huntspill with East Huntspill | |
| 1983–91 | James Hill | Death |
| 1991–94 | Christopher Hudson | Resignation |
| 1994– | Geoffrey Walsh | Resignation |

*Note:*
*'Death' = death of previous incumbent*
*'Cession' = vacating one living by accepting another*

# MASONIC HISTORY IN THE CHURCHYARD

The tombstone of John Jennings, which stands within ten yards of the bell-tower steps in West Huntspill churchyard, is of considerable interest as the lower six lines are engraved in a Masonic cipher script. The headstone commemorates a man who, in 1793, was one of the founder members of the 'Masonic Rural Philanthropic Lodge', which subsequently met regularly at Highbridge Inn (at the time within the parish of West Huntspill). John Jennings was an architect and land surveyor who, in 1779, undertook to repair the river gates and lock on the Brue at Highbridge. He lost over £100 of his own money fulfilling this contract and it would seem that he wished to immortalise this fact by arranging to have details inscribed on his headstone which, incidentally, was part of the original lock.

The cipher is based on two of the Masonic codes, the square and the compass. The square denotes square or good conduct and the compass signifies keeping within or encompassing God's law. Letters A–R are based on the square while the letters S–Z depict the arms of a compass. Either two or three sides of a square denote the first four characters of the alphabet, with E being the completed square. The letters F, G, H and I are an inverted image of D, C, B and A. The letters J–R are the same letters as A–I with a dot in the centre of the square. The symbols for the letters S, T, U and V are repeated for W, X, Y and Z with a dot in their centre. The translation of the script reads:

*This stone is part of the apron or floor of Highbridge, which being much broken and in vain attempted to be repaired for sixty years, was completely repaired in the year 1779 by John Jennings, who lost £100 by doing it.*

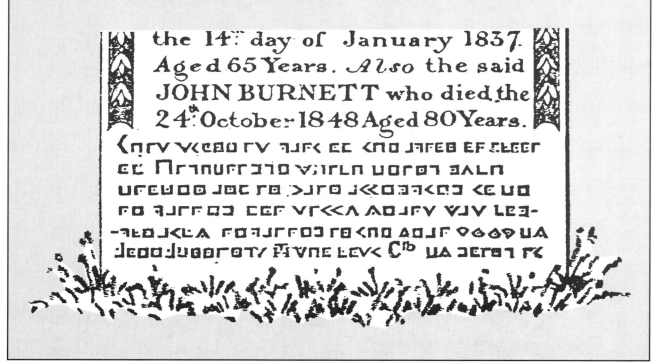

## DESTRUCTION OF ST PETER'S BY FIRE
(Somerset County Gazette, *14 December 1878*)

*Early on Monday morning St. Peter's Church Huntspill, near Bridgwater, and one of the largest Parishes in the Bridgwater Union, was discovered to be on fire, and, in a few hours afterwards, nothing but the bare walls remained of what was considered to be, in all respects, one of the best Churches in Somerset. So recently as last Easter, the Church, which is a good example of the late Perpendicular style, was re-opened by the Bishop of the Diocese, assisted by Archdeacon Dennison, after the completion of a restoration which had cost more than £1,500.*

*Between two and three o'clock, the Rev. W.O. Wilson, the newly appointed Rector, was alarmed by a peculiar noise, and he perceived from his bedroom window at the Rectory nearby, that the roof of the Sacred Edifice was on fire.*

*He quickly raised an alarm and many of the parishioners were soon on the spot. When the roof started to fall in, the Rector cautioned the men who were helping to remove things from the Church, and who had already secured the chest containing the vestry books and Parish registers, lectern and portions of the pulpit and Altar, not to re-enter the Church, and soon after the roof fell in bodily.*

*Some time elapsed before the arrival of the West of England Fire Brigade, when efforts were made to save the chancel and tower, the former containing a magnificent stained-glass window, erected by the family of a former Rector (Rev. N.T. Ellison) and the latter a remarkably fine peal of bells. It was soon apparent however that their efforts would prove unsuccessful, and, the ringing floor having first given way, the bells soon followed, four of them breaking in pieces and smashing a beautiful font on which they fell, the remaining two being very much smashed.*

*The Church walls had upon them some beautiful tablets, and the interior was lighted by means of a very valuable chandelier, the gift of a former Rector.*

*An interior view of the church, roofless, after the fire of 1878.*

*Fragment of the church floor tile found in the churchyard, possibly thrown out after the fire of 1878.*

*West Huntspill bells and ringers at the foot of the tower, 1953.*
Left to right: *Mervyn Farthing, Jim Farthing, Harry Parkhouse, Bert Turner, Jack Baker, Revd Morgan, Jack Hobbs, Wilf Parkhouse, Mr Cox, Mr Greener, Donald Harding.*

# Church Bells

Before 1877 a mixed ring of five bells was hung in the tower. Their numbers and corresponding inscriptions were:

### No. 1
*Mr Charles Colston & Mr James Saunders
Church Wardens 1732 Cast by Thos Bilbie*

### No. 2
*Mr Samuel Jeffery Mr Thos Strange
Churchwardens 1753
'Health, Wealth and Peace to this Neighbourhood'
Cast by Bayley Street & Co.*

### No. 3
*Mr Thomas Greenwood Churchwarden
Thomas Bilbie
Cullompton Fecit 1790*

### No. 4
*William Body John Glandfield
Anno Domini 1693*

### No. 5
*'God Save the Queen & Church'
Geo White Church Warden 1704
Alun Rudhall Gloucester
Bellfounder*

**The church clock is inscribed with the words:**

*Church Clock Made in 1687
Robert Came Thomas Robsalt Churchwardens
also New Quarter Clock £43.10s.7d. in 1747*

The five bells were recast in 1877, but during the disastrous fire on 9 December 1878 the heat was so intense that the bells were melted. The following appeared in the *Huntspill News* during 1977:

*About ten days ago a Mr Stanley Jordan of Coventry telephoned the Rectory to let us know that he had in his possession a gong made from the Huntspill bells which were melted by the fire in 1878. On September 22nd he came with his wife, Joy, to present this interesting gong to the Church. We know only of one other in the possession of Mrs D.V. House, which she tells us was given to her by a member of the Burnett family, once well known in this village. We are indeed most grateful to Mr & Mrs Jordan for their kind gift and hope to find a use for it on suitable occasions.*

In 1879 six new bells were cast as follows:

*The bell tower.*

> J Taylor & Co. Founders
> Loughborough 1879
> W.O. Wilson, Rector
> John Burnett
> Edwin Vowles
> Churchwardens 1879

These bells were re-hung in 1953 on ball-bearings and iron headstocks. Their measurements are:

| No | Diameter | Note | Weight cwt/lbs/oz. |
|---|---|---|---|
| Treble | 2' 8⅜" | C sharp | 7-1-19 |
| 2 | 2' 10¼" | B | 8-0-2 |
| 3 | 3' 1½" | A | 10-0-20 |
| 4 | 3' 3¼" | G sharp | 11-2-12 |
| 5 | 3' 7⅝" | F sharp | 14-1-8 |
| 6 | 4' 1⅜" | E | 22-3-24 |

*Bell-ringers, c.1940.  Left to right: Tony Fackrell, Stan Chedgey, Bert Turner and Mr Aish.*

*West Huntspill Bell-ringers, 1978.* Left to right, back row: *Madge Langdon, Charles Langdon, ?, ?, ?;* front: *David Holley, ?, ?, Revd Alun Virgin, Alan Jones, Jenefer Tiley, ?.*

One Christmas Day in the 1960s, the clapper on the tenor bell broke in half. The village blacksmith, Mr Harding, rectified the problem and by Boxing Day it had been refitted good as new!

In those days it was the usual practice for the ringers to ring for two hours on Boxing Day working off the Christmas turkey! The following reference to bell-ringing activities during 1975 is quoted from the *Huntspill News:*

*1975 has been quite an eventful year, started off by 'ringing out the old and ringing in the new', according to tradition. Later in January a demonstration of bell-ringing was given to some of the pupils of West Huntspill school, who in return sent a nice letter of thanks to the Tower Captain. During February a quarter peal of 'Beverley Surprise Minor' was rung by a team consisting of ringers from Bridgwater and Bristol areas. The sad loss of the Revd RCV Hodge in March was followed by a memorial, half-muffled quarter peal, rung in the evening of the day of his interment. We were grateful to two ringers from Wembdon who stood in at short notice to make this possible. Details of this tribute are recorded in the belfry. The Branch Striking Contest in April was at Nether Stowey. West Huntspill entered and came in fifth place with 24 faults. Quite a busy day as the same team rang for a wedding at Huntspill before*

*ringing at Nether Stowey. We welcomed a visiting team from Essex in May. The men working on the tower stonework said the bells would not interfere with them and even left off working while ringing was in progress. They must have been good sports! The Bath & Wells Association had their monthly midweek evening practice at Huntspill in June and a variety of methods were rung to cater for all tastes, under the direction of the Branch Ringing Master and his deputy. Visitors from Deal, Kent, joined our ringers to ring for Morning Service on the first Sunday in July and afterwards attended the Family Service. An outing to John Taylor's Bell Foundry at Loughborough in August enabled us to see casting in progress and to ring on the foundry bells – a 6cwt ring of ten – an experience for those used to 'the heavies'. Also worthy of mention in August was the quarter peal rung to mark the beginning of the Festival of Joy events. This was achieved by the regular Sunday Service ringers of Huntspill. Several tied practices were held during the months of September and October to encourage new recruits to the art of bell control. A quarter peal attempt in November was lost in the last sixty changes. We hope to make another attempt at a later date. December is always a busy month for ringers everywhere. Christmas bells send out their joyous message. The Huntspill team certainly did*

*Millennium Bell-ringers, 2000.*
Left to right: *Alan Jones, Marion Newman, Colin Bird, Nathanial Bird,*
*Peter Leigh, Richard Tiley, Janet Hockaday, Christine Tiley, Madge Langdon, Charlie Langdon.*

*just that this Christmas. Team spirit is what counts in the tower and bell-ringing, as many newcomers have found, is a very fascinating and rewarding hobby.*

The following are further quotes from the *Huntspill News* of the period:

*Huntspill has long been noted for its church bells which, apart from their enforced silence during the war years, have rung out over the surrounding district for many decades, a performance which could not have been maintained without that dedicated body of people, its bellringers. One of these who springs to mind from earlier days was Mr Bill Sellick, for many years... Captain of bellringers in the days of Revd. Pizey. In his later years he had great difficulty in climbing the stairway to the tower and finally relinquished the post which was taken on by Mr Bert Turner. In his everyday life Mr Sellick kept a cycle repair shop opposite the chapel... [see Chapter One]*

*A quarter peal and a peal on the same day? – this was achieved on Jubilee Day by West Huntspill and Bridgwater Branch Ringers in honour of the 25 years' reign of Her Majesty Queen Elizabeth II.*

*During the morning a successful quarter peal of 'Plain Bob Doubles' was rung in 48 minutes, being 1260 changes. The ringers were: Ruth Gregory (Treble), Mrs M. Langdon (2), C. Langdon (3), R. Tiley (4), A. Jones (5), R. Brooks (Tenor). They were conducted by A. Jones. In the afternoon a peal of 'Plain Bob Minor' was rung. It was the first on the bells for 23 years (the last peal having been rung in 1954 to commemorate the safe homecoming of the Queen from her Commonwealth tour). This was achieved in three hours and three minutes, being 5040 changes. The ringers were: R. Tiley (Treble), A. Jones (2), C. Harris (3), C. Clarke (4), E. Dibble (5), M. Stone (Tenor). They were conducted by M. Stone. Congratulations to Richard Tiley on ringing his first peal.*

*History was also made since this was the first peal of minor on the bells (minor being a method with all six bells changing places). The previous three peals rung at Huntspill, in 1904, 1956 and 1954, were doubles, i.e. with the Tenor covering.*

At the time of writing in 2001, the West Huntspill Bell-ringers are: C. Bird, A. Jones, C. Langdon, Mrs M. Langdon, Mrs C. Tiley, R. Tiley (Captain).

## Church Music

*Choristers at St Peter's, 1940s. John Holley is second from the right.*

*A wedding party with the choir outside the Old Rectory, 1940s.*

## Church Music

*Huntspill Choir, c.1876.*

*Church Choir, early 1900s.*

## *Methodism*

*The Methodist Chapel, 1860.*

*Main Road with the Methodist Chapel and Globe Hotel, c.1900.*

*Chapter Four*

# METHODISM

There were Protestant Dissenters in the village during the late 1790s, but the earliest reference to a local Methodist applying for a licence to use his home as a meeting-place for fellow worshippers was in July 1802. This was William Cooper who was supported by two of the Burnett family, among others. John Wesley had journeyed through the village en route from Bridgwater to Brent Knoll in September 1769. Possibly a number of the local people had been influenced by his preaching at Bridgwater on one of the three occasions that he visited that town.

People from all sectors of society, from labourers to gentlemen, were attracted to the Methodist cause and many of them wished to worship in their own homes, although by 1826 11 members of the Bible Christian faith were worshipping in East Huntspill.

The chapel in West Huntspill was built on land given by Edwin Budge, a blacksmith, whose shop was adjacent to the chosen site. The total cost of the building was £335 and the first service took place some time in 1851. There was no mention of it in the local Bridgwater paper, nor does there appear to be any surviving record of the official opening in the Bridgwater Circuit records. Income was mainly derived from seat rents, which netted around £11 annually during the first decade of worship.

Prominent amongst the early members were most of the Tilley family, who lived, at various times, in Huntspill Court, Alstone Court and New Road Farm, and Charles Churchill, a local saddler. In the early years of the last century, if one was not in the chapel a half hour or so before the start of the main festival services, such as Christmas, Easter and Harvest, then you would have had to stand in the aisles or the entrance porch. At that time there were almost 100 scholars in ten classes of the Sunday School and they had free access to a library of 160 books: even in the 1950s and early '60s the Sunday School was strongly supported.

Members of the Cavill family have been major mainstays of chapel life for almost a century now and

*The Methodist Chapel and Globe Hotel, late 1940s.*

*Interior of Methodist Chapel before renovations, 1996.*

*The Methodist Chapel pulpit prior to the restoration in 1996.*

*The Methodist Chapel renovations, 1996.
Removing the old timber floor. Wood
estimated to be 600–700 years old was
discovered in the floor and may have
come from an old barn.*

*The service conducted after
the 1996 renovations.
Left to right, back row:
J. Lamb, W. Watts, M. Watts,
Revd M. Adams, D. Manning,
M. Thomas, M. Waterhouse,
J. O'Neill, M. Moreton,
G. Slocombe;
front: R. Stuart, J. Pearce,
C. Thomas, ?, A. Thomas,
?, I. Hawkes, C. Withers.*

three generations have served the Circuit faithfully as lay preachers. The nearby Ilex Nurseries were owned by them from 1900. Wesley and Ivy and their father, Frank, were local preachers in the Bridgwater Circuit. Frank would often walk or cycle to Pawlett Hams and catch the ferry boat to take him across the River Parrett to preach a service at Combwich. There has been only one burial in the grounds of the chapel and that was in 1890 when one of the founder members, William Tilley of Alstone Court, was laid to rest.

The schoolroom was in an upstairs room at the back of the church and underneath were stables where the visiting preacher could put his horse whilst the service was taking place. This was demolished in 1976 and a new single-storey extension built. The gallery in the church has a lovely organ which has been played lovingly by many people including Elsie Fisher and Joyce Toogood. New windows were installed for the centenary donated by Walter Clark in memory of his wife.

In 1995 the bold decision was taken to remove all the pews to provide a versatile area for general community activities. Whilst this work was being undertaken, some extraordinary timber joists were discovered supporting the floor boarding. This bevelled and painted timber, which was secured with what looked like horseshoe nails and laid across earth-based brick pillars three or four feet apart, obviously came from a building of substance which must have been demolished around the time when the chapel was first planned. A portion from one of these timbers is, at the time of writing, being treering-dated at Sheffield University and it will be interesting to see how accurate the estimates of 600–700 years old are when the results have been obtained. Also discovered at the same time were several air vents embedded in the outside walls below floor level, together with two pipes for supplying gas to two wall-mounted gas heaters, which were used until they were replaced by the current electric heaters.

The stained glass in the screen just in front of the entrance was taken down and incorporated in the new screen. Being fairly fragile, this was protected by clear glass on both sides. The new screen has been placed further forward which has increased the size of the entrance hall enabling it to be used also as an extra space. Concrete was laid to a depth which adequately covered the brick pillars mentioned above, and this in turn was then covered with various layers of damp-proof membrane before being finished with a cement screed.

The old side panelling was replaced with tongue-and-groove timber, complete with dado rail along the top; the whole being lightly varnished. The walls were repainted and toning wall-to-wall carpeting laid. To replace the pews (which were sold to a firm in Salisbury), 36 individual, but interlocking, upholstered chairs (some with arms) were purchased which allows the seating to be adapted to the occasion. A finely produced cross was made from the wood of one of the pitch-pine pew panels and placed in the centre recess of the west wall. This cross was executed by John Davey who, with his assistants, undertook and completed the refurbishment.

John also renovated the hymn board, which together with a new set of numbers, usually ensures that the latter stay in place without any artificial assistance such as gum or bluetak! The entrance has been provided with a ramp which makes access easier for disabled visitors. The communion rail has been redesigned using some of the original cast-iron supports, and two handmade wooden collection plates were made locally. A time capsule including a plan of the church with pews, a Wesleyan Chapel cup and saucer and a copy of Concord was placed in the wall behind the pulpit. The Seekers (a youth group) also prepared a time capsule which contained a photograph and a short autobiographical piece about each member of the group, together with newspaper cuttings and tickets, programmes, etc. dating back to 1901. There are also copies of photographs taken during the 1993 Flower Festival.

In 2001 the chapel celebrates its 150th anniversary with flowers, music and craft. A special celebration cake is being cut by the great-granddaughter of William Tilley. Since the refurbishments have been made the building has been used for various functions and the congregation are now able to sit on comfortable chairs instead of hard pews and enjoy modern comforts without losing the character of the building which our descendants provided for us.

## Chapter Five
# SCHOOLS & THE BALLIOL HALL

There have been a number of schools in the village. The predecessor of the present primary school on New Road was the schoolroom at the Balliol Hall. This is believed to date from 1828 although there was a redevelopment of the building in 1876. There is in existence, dated 1815, a set of School Rules for a charity school. These may appertain to the school James Jennings set up with the help of the rector, Mr How, in 1813, along the lines of the monitorial system of Andrew Bell. Tuition was free, but no child whose parents were able to pay for education were admitted and the establishment was financed by voluntary subscriptions. A subscriber had the right to nominate pupils in number according to the size of their subscription. The following are transcripts of the (breathless) Indentures (originals held by the Somerset County Records Office) which enabled the establish-

ment of the schools in 1828 and 1876. Punctuation is made prominent by its total absence:

*This Indenture made this tenth day of March in the year of our Lord one thousand eight hundred and twenty eight Between the Reverend Noel Thomas Ellison Rector of the Parish of Huntspill in the County of Somerset Clerk of the one part and the Reverend Richard Jenkyns Doctor in Divinity and Master of Balliol College Oxford Nathaniel Ellison of Upper Bedford Place in the County of Middlesex Esquire and Joseph Ruscombe Poole of Bridgwater in the County of Somerset Gentleman of the other part Whereas the said Noel Thomas Ellison is seized in Fee of the Schoolhouse and premises hereinafter described and hereinafter demised or otherwise assured or so intended to be and hath agreed that the same shall be demised unto the said*

*View from the church tower looking east, 1860s. Visible are the three cottages on School Lane (entrance to Balliol Hall) and the roof of the school, built in 1828, to the right.*

*The school in the 1930s.*

Richard Jenkyns Nathaniel Ellison and Joseph Ruscombe Poole their Executors Administrators and assigns for the Term hereinafter mentioned upon the Trusts and to and for the intents and purposes hereinafter expressed and declared of and concerning the same From this Indenture Witnesseth that in pursuance of the said Agreement and in Consideration of the sum of ten shillings of lawful money of the United Kingdom of Great Britain and Ireland current in Great Britain to the said Noel Thomas Ellison at or before the sealing and delivery of these presents in hand paid by the said Richard Jenkyns Nathaniel Ellison and Joseph Ruscombe Poole the receipt whereof is hereby acknowledged He the said Noel Thomas Ellison Hath granted bargained sold demised and confirmed and by these presents Doth grant bargain sell demise and confirm unto the said Richard Jenkyns Nathaniel Ellison and Joseph Ruscombe Poole their Executors Administrators and assigns All that Schoolhouse which hath been newly erected by the said Noel Thomas Ellison on a plot of Ground whereon a Cottage or Dwellinghouse lately stood situate near the Churchyard of Huntspill aforesaid bounded on the West by the said Churchyard on the East by a Road leading to a Close of Land belonging to the Rectory of Huntspill on the south by the same Close of Land and on the North by a stable which said Noel Thomas Ellison purchased the same in fee simple as may appear Together with all Houses outhouses edifices Buildings Courts ways paths passages waters watercourses easements profits commodities appertaining To have and to hold the said Schoolhouse and premises hereinbefore demised and granted or so intended to be

with the appurtenances unto the said Richard Jenkyns Nathaniel Ellison and Joseph Ruscombe Poole their Executors Administrators and Assigns from henceforth for and during and unto the full end and Term of Ten Thousand Years Fully to be complete and ended Yielding and paying therefore unto the said Noel Thomas Ellison his Heirs and Assigns yearly and every year during the said Term the Rent of a pepper Corn at the Feast of Saint Michael the Archangel if lawfully demanded And the said Noel Thomas Ellison doth hereby declare direct and appoint that the said Richard Jenkyns Nathaniel Ellison and Joseph Ruscombe Poole their Executors Administrators and assigns shall stand and be possessed of and interested in the said Schoolhouse and premises hereinbefore described and hereby demised or intended so to be Upon the Trusts and to and for the intents and purposes hereinafter expressed and declared concerning the same that is to say Upon Trust that they the said Richard Jenkyns Nathaniel Ellison and Joseph Ruscombe Poole and the survivors and survivor of them and the Executors Administrators and Assigns of such Survivor do and shall from time to time and at all times hereafter permit and suffer the said Schoolhouse and premises to be used and occupied under the Entire and exclusive direction and control of the Rector for the time being of the Parish of Huntspill aforesaid as and for a Schoolhouse for receiving the Poor Inhabitants of the said Parish of Huntspill therein on Sundays and other Days in order to their being instructed in Religious and other useful learning Provided always and it is hereby declared to be the intent and meaning of the said parties hereto *that the Master or Mistress of the School which shall be kept in the said schoolhouse hereby demised shall be appointed by the Rector of the time being of the said Parish of Huntspill and that such school Master or School Mistress shall hold his or her Office during the pleasure of such Rector and no longer And the said Noel Thomas Ellison doth hereby for himself his Heirs Executors and Administrators Covenant promise and agree to and with the said Richard Jenkyns Nathaniel Ellison and Joseph Ruscombe Poole and each of then their and each of their Executors and Administrators in manner following that is to say That the said Schoolhouse and premises hereinbefore mentioned to be hereby demised and granted or so intended to be with the appurtenances shall and lawfully may from time to time and at all times hereafter remain continue and be vested in the said Richard Jenkyns Nathaniel Ellison and Joseph Ruscombe Poole their Executors Administrators and assigns to and for the uses upon the Trusts and for the ends intents and purposes hereinbefore mentioned expressed and declared of and concerning the same without any let sint hinderance interruption or denial whatsoever of or by the said Noel Thomas Ellison his Heirs Executors Administrators or Assigns or any other person or persons whomsoever having or lawfully claiming or who shall or may have or lawfully claim any Estate right tithe Trust or Interest of into or out of the same Premises or any part or parcel thereof by from through under or in Trust for him or them In Witness whereof the said parties to these presents have hereinto set their hands and Seals the day and year first above written.*

The second Indenture reads:

*THIS INDENTURE made the .......... day of ......... 1874 Between The Reverend James Gylby Lonsdale, Clerk of the Rectory of Huntspill in the County of Somerset and Diocese of Bath and Wells of the 1st part The Master of Scholars of Balliol College in the University of Oxford the Patrons of the Rectory of Huntspill aforesaid of the 2nd. part The Hon. Right Revd Arthur Charles Lord Bishop of the said Diocese of Bath and Wells of the 3rd part Edward Saunders o' Huntspill aforesaid. Gentleman of the 4th part and The Rector Churchwardens and Overseers of the Parish of Huntspill aforesaid of the 5th part Witnessed that under the authority of the Acts of the 5th and 8th years of the Reign of Her Majesty Queen Victoria for affording facilities for the Conveyance and Endowment of sites for Schools He the said James Gylby Lonsdale as the Rector of the Rectory aforesaid with the consent of the said Master and Scholars of Balliol College aforesaid as such Patrons as aforesaid and of the said Arthur Charles Lord Bishop of the Diocese aforesaid testified by their execution of these presents Doth freely and voluntarily and without valuable consideration grant and convey unto the said Edward Saunders and his heirs All That the School*

*house of Huntspill aforesaid with the plot, piece or parcel of land forming the site thereof adjoining the Churchyard there and in the Tithe Map of Huntspill aforesaid included in such Churchyard which is No. 294 on the same map AND ALSO ALL THAT plot piece or parcel of land part of a Close of Ground called the three acres and No. 300 on the said Tithe Map which said Schoolhouse plots pieces or parcels of Ground and premises intended to be hereby granted and conveyed are situate in the Parish of Huntspill aforesaid and are parcels of the Glebe lands of the said Rectory of Huntspill and are delineated and coloured pink on the plan drawn in the margin of these presents Together with all houses, easements and appurtenances to the same belonging AND the reversion and reversions ...... and ...... rents issues and profits thereof AND all the estate and interest of the said Rector of Huntspill therein TO HAVE and to hold the said School house plots pieces and parcels of ground and premises with the appurtenances unto the said Edward Saunders and his heirs Nevertheless TO the use of the Rector Churchwardens and Overseers of the Parish of Huntspill aforesaid and their successors for ever UPON TRUST To permit the said plots pieces or parcels of land intended to be hereby granted and conveyed and the said Schoolhouse and buildings now standing thereon and all further buildings which shall be hereafter erected thereon or on any part thereof to be for ever hereafter appropriated and used as a School for the education of Children and Adults or Children only of the labouring manufacturing and industrial Classes of the Parish of Huntspill aforesaid subject to the declarations and provisions hereinafter contained that is to say PROVIDED always and it is hereby declared that such School shall be at all times open to the inspection of the Inspector of Schools appointed or to be appointed by the Education Department of Her Majesty's Privy Council or by the Bishop for the time being of the Diocese of Bath and Wells aforesaid and shall always be in union with and conducted according to the principles of the National Society for promoting the Education of the Poor in the principles of the Established Church in England and Wales and such school and premises and income thereof shall be controlled and managed in manner following that is to say The Rector of Huntspill for the time being or his licensed Curate shall have the superintendence at all times of the religious instruction of the Scholars attending such School and may use the premises as a Sunday School under the control and management but in all other respects the control and management of the School and of the funds and income thereof and the selection appointment and dismissal of the Schoolmaster and Schoolmistress and of their respective Assistants shall be vested in and exercised by a Committee consisting of the said Rector his licensed Curate, or Curates and seventeen or any less number of persons to be elected by the persons who shall have been subscribers to such School to the* mount of 10/— at least for twelve months previously to the day of election and such Committee shall be elected annually at some meeting of the Subscribers which shall be held in each year for the audit of the accounts of the preceding year but in the event of any neglect to appoint and Committee the Committee who shall have acted during the preceding year shall continue in office Provided always that no such selection appointment or dismissal as aforesaid shall at any time or times be made unless the Rector for the time being of the said Parish of Huntspill shall consent thereto in writing Provided also that the Master and Mistress of the said School and their assistants shall respectfully be members of the Established Church of England In witness etc. Perused and Settled on behalf of The Lord Bishop of Bath & Wells

**(Signed) Bernard.**
**Wells 23rd. Feb. 1874.**

Other educational establishments included a private school at Swell House which was owned by the Burnett family who also owned the Ilex Stores.

A Miss Bacon ran a kindergarten at the house on the corner of Church Road and Silver Street at c.1900. The present primary school dates from 1897 and was formally opened on 10 January 1898. It was sited to be equidistant between the main village and South Highbridge so that infants did not have too far to walk. The following is quoted from the *Bridgwater Mercury* (December 1896):

*At a meeting of the school board held on Friday week, it was agreed to accept the tender of Mr H.W. Pollard of Bridgwater, for the erection of new Board Schools for West Huntspill and Highbridge at a cost not exceeding £3,000.*

In January 1898 the following was reported:

*Opening of a new board of schools – The School Board for the combined parish of East and West Huntspill and South Highbridge must be congratulated on their completion of the new school buildings at West Huntspill, which were formally opened by the chairman Mr Henry Tilley of Alstone Court. The newly erected schools have been built close to the main highway, a suitable piece of land having been purchased from Mr Toogood by Mr H.W. Pollard of Bridgwater whose contract amounted to £3,120 from designs prepared by Mr A. Basil Cottam the board's architect also of Bridgwater and Taunton. They consist of commodious schools and playground and some land has also been fenced in for the master's residence.*

The Headmaster from the turn of the century was Norman Reynolds who served until 1915 when he was called up to serve in the war.

A Sergeant in the 8th Battalion Somerset Light Infantry, he was reported missing in France on 25 September that year. The school staff at the time were recorded as:

**Certified**
Norman Reynolds, Annual salary £175
Gladys Reynolds, Annual salary £95

**Uncertified**
Winnie Brown, Annual salary £50
Nellie Holwill, Annual salary £50
Millicent Thompson, Annual salary £45
Eva Winslade, Annual salary £30
Gladys Baker, Annual salary £6.10s.0d.

**Total salaries: £451.10s.0d.**

The roll of headmasters at the school reads as follows:

1902–15   Norman Reynolds
1915–55   Lionel Davey
1956–64   Mr Eastlake
1964–84   Peter Powell
1984–88   Margaret Ralph
1989–      Paul Flux

The following is taken from an issue of the *Huntspill News* from the mid 1970s:

*One of those whose name is still mentioned with respect by many and who gave a great deal of colour to Huntspill in earlier years was Mr L.A. Davey, Headmaster of Huntspill School (pictured inset), a man who made a great impact on several generations. He was a man of many parts, sportsman, historian, church organist, teacher and entertainer (there must be many who can recall his rendering of the 'Jan Stewar' tales told in a rich Devonshire dialect!), but above all there was his ability to control and command the respect of the children in his care whilst his maintenance of discipline was something which would be an even greater asset in the present day. His authority did not end at the school gates either, the sight of his robust figure cycling along the main road was enough to*

*turn any would-be vandals into models of propriety! He was a man who could assert his authority, and although on occasions was known to use the cane, his voice and command of adjectives would usually subdue any dissident pupil. It is worth mentioning that the children in his care came from an area covering Woolavington, Dunball, East and West Huntspill up to the age of 14 years but he coped with them all. Parents, too, accepted his role of authority and were content to leave it at that. He was truly 'one of the old school'.*

And this is a poem written by a pupil of Mr Davey:

Mr Davey is a very nice man who
goes to church on Sundays
to pray for strength to wallop the kids on Mondays.
But if by chance he cannot go owing to rain,
he loses his pluck and cannot hold the cane.
But if he finds he is in a fix he goes and calls for aid
and then we get our punishment
from dear old Tommy Wade.

Corporal punishment was of course part of the rigour of school life until the early 1950s when we entered more 'enlightened' times!

## EXTRACTS FROM THE SCHOOL PUNISHMENT REGISTER

### 1908

| DATE | NAME | OFFENCE | PUNISHMENT |
|---|---|---|---|
| 3rd Sept. | Meaker, A. | Laziness | 2 on back |
| | Sheer, W. | Laziness | 2 on hand |
| 4th Sept. | Keylock, G. | Troublesome | 1 on back |
| | Channon, W. | Talking | 2 on hand |
| | Parkhouse, C. | Loitering | 1 on back |
| | Fry, P. | Loitering | 1 on back |
| 8th Sept. | Webb, H. | Troublesome | 2 on hands |
| | Lynham, V. | Troublesome | 2 on hands |
| 10th Sept. | Turner, A. | Disobedience | Some on back |
| | Beasley, V. | Troublesome | 2 on back |
| | Wright, S. | Troublesome | 1 on back |
| 14th Sept. | Fry, P. | Careless Work | 1 on back |

The records continue with punishments inflicted on a daily basis (girls included) for such misdemeanours as 'truanting', 'stealing apples', 'walking on desks', 'punching other girls' and 'playing'. Punishments continued until after the Second World War, but on a more infrequent basis. The last entries were for 1953:

| DATE | NAME | OFFENCE | PUNISHMENT |
|---|---|---|---|
| 1953 | Gordon Turner | Entering a shop on way to Woodwork and becoming a nuisance | 2 on hands |
| | Brian Lloyd } Peter Moran } | Interfering with Bakery door on way back from Woodwork | 1 on hand 2 on hands |

## Down through the years

*The school in April, 1912, headmaster Norman Reynolds at the right, rear.*

*West Huntspill School group, c.1916.  Left to right, back row: Harry Knights, ?, Herbert Wilkins, Len Foster,
Jack Lawless, Eddie Burchell, Herbert Harding; 4th row: Jack Swain, Cyril Parish, Ron Bastin, ?, Reggie Hancock, Wilfred
Hawkings, Teddy Toogood; 3rd row: Liz Tanner, Joyce Cavill, Kathy Lane, Doris Davis; 2nd row: Eiliffe Amesbury, ?
Holley, L.A. Davey, Ruby Hayes, Edwina Tanner; front: ? Solomon, Hedley Jones, Lionel Hawkings, Vivienne Foster.*

## *Down through the years*

*West Huntspill School, Infants Class, early 1920s.*
*The children in the photo include Reg Hooper, Stan Chedgey, Betty Foster and Freda Derham.*

*School gardening class, 1920s.*

## Down through the years

*West Huntspill School, 1920 or 1921.  The teacher is Miss Storey.*
*The children include: Wyndham Watts, Fred Chedgey, George Woolley and Cecil Brown.*

*West Huntspill School, early 1920s.  The child in the centre of the third row is thought to be Thelma Hooper.*

## Down through the years

*West Huntspill School, 1931.* Children in class include: *Vince Derham, Eddie Ham, Bob Thorn, Ray Hawkins, Bruce Haggett, Audrey Bishop, Stella Holley, Doris Difford, Gordon Coombes, Geoff Styles, Gerald Puddy, Geoffrey Hardwidge, ? Burfitt, June Whitcombe, June Farrow, Mary Sandy, Peter Slocombe, Jack Foster, Tony Braund and Karen Bidgood.*

*School group, 1935.*

## *Down through the years*

*West Huntspill School, 1949.  Left to right, back row: C. Brown, T. Burridge, E. Hooper, K. Cunningham, P. Bishop, J. Bell, B. Allen, G. Thorne, T. Lee; middle row: T. Difford, J. Marsh, G. Saunders, C. Reason, J. Watts, S. Pomeroy, J. Mockridge, J. Saunders, T. Stevens; front: J. Cox, J. Fowler, S. Bennett, ? Brown, K. Solomon, J. Garrett, G. Bellamy, R. Kingston, P. Hand, J. Taylor, K. Riddle.  The teacher, standing to the right, is Miss Cox.*

*Staff and School Governors, 1950s.*

*West Huntspill County Primary School, 1981. Members of staff (teaching and non-teaching), from the left:*
*Peter Powell (headmaster), Betty Lambert, Pat Harvey, Lin Gardner, Ann Thomas, Ann Jarvis, Mrs Solomon,*
*Barbara Bennett, Martin Atton, Audrey Rogers, Ruth Edkins, Pat Pennington, Sue Walsh and Freda Richardson.*

Much of the work done by the community to aid the school is voluntary. This also includes the Parent Teacher Association. As ever, school budgets in the 1970s were tight and fund-raising and self-help were a feature of their activities. The following account of the effort to supply a new school library in 1977 testifies to this:

*The new School Library was formally opened at a meeting held on the evening of June 21st. The Headmaster, Mr. Powell, expressed his gratitude for all the goodwill and co-operation the School had received over the years and welcomed Mr. Derek Esp, Deputy Chief Education Officer for Somerset, and Mr. Neil Widgery, Area Education Officer. The Secretary of the Parent-Teachers' Association, Mrs. Olwyn McCormack, expressed the regret of the meeting at the enforced absence of Mr. Barry Taylor, Chief Education Officer, and asked Mr. Esp to convey to him the thanks of all concerned for his kindly encouragement and good wishes. She then gave a very interesting and detailed account of the history of this project, now so successfully completed.*

*The Library Project was first initiated in 1972. At this particular time, with 180 children in the school, it was felt that an additional teaching space in the form of a library-cum-quiet-room would alleviate the difficulties being experienced by a class of some 30 children working in extremely cramped and confined conditions. The initial response from County Hall, Taunton, for assistance with a self-help project, was not at all encouraging – in fact it was not until Mr Widgery called into the school one day that the scene was finally set and the wheels put in motion. Within the space of six months £1000 had been set aside by County Hall for the library project, plus the promise of all possible help from the Architects' Department in the purchase of materials and, eventually, the most suitable methods of paying bills to avoid VAT. The Parents' Committee are fully aware of the interest that was shown by Neil Widgery in the opening stages of the library development and all would wish it recorded that he did good work on their behalf and offer him sincere thanks for his help and interest.*

*Early in 1975 it was agreed that Mr John Marsh should be put in charge of the development and by*

*June the plans for the library had been drawn by Mr John Davey and submitted to the Architects' Department, and later the Planning Department. Permission to start building was given on 23 August 1976. At this stage, John Marsh and Partners Ltd. thought it appropriate to start placing orders for building materials, mainly owing to rising prices, although it was not intended that building should begin until early spring 1977. Nearly all the materials were purchased through Shepherd Brothers of Highbridge, and the school obtained a most generous discount. In March 1977 a start was made on the foundations and a pneumatic drill, complete with compressor was hired. Thus three teachers, plus Mr. Marsh, Mr. Bishop and Mr. Broom, commenced work on a certain Saturday morning. The drill proved a somewhat startling innovation for the teaching staff who, by lunch time were visibly shaken. Nevertheless the trench visibly deepened. By mid-afternoon conversation became limited and the fatigue of hard physical graft was becoming apparent to the uninitiated. In fact it was some weeks after this traumatic experience that our then Deputy Head, Mr. Speakman, successfully applied for another teaching post on the upper reaches of Exmoor and hasn't been seen since!*

*Our special thanks are also due to Gordon Lockyer for the loan of his tractor and trailer to carry away the debris and rubble. It wasn't long before the foundations had been inspected, passed and duly concreted in. By April 10th the brickwork was due to start and on this Saturday morning Mr. Gardner and Mr. Close erected the entire front of the building, beginning at 8a.m. and finishing at noon. Both parents and staff became mortar mixers, hod carriers and general useless advisors to the experts. The next stage in the proceedings involved the removal of the vast blocks of ornamental Ham stone (each weighing several hundredweights) from the tops of the doorways that had for so many years designated the separate openings for 'Girls' and 'Infants'. Mr. Powell says that these monumental blocks are now available for disposal to anyone interested. Mr. John Davey, with the help of Mr. Trevor Lee, next constructed the roof timbers, fastened the chipboard sheets and sent for a firm of tarmacadam and felting experts to finish covering the roof. The library windows are of anodised aluminium and were the most generous gift of Mr. Stan Johnson of West Huntspill, who fitted them into the existing timber frames and also glazed the double doors and windows at the back of the hall. During the Summer Holidays Mr. John Thorne rendered and plastered the walls, ceiling, and the two small attractive panels on the exterior walls of the Library. We suppose that the materials involved for plastering were, like the windows, a gift, for no mention has ever been made of these additional expenses or of the long hours spent on our behalf. The electrical side of the project was admirably accomplished by Mr. Mike Jones, who, although complaining that he was really only a T.V. engineer, managed to finish a splendid job.*

*The school under water during the flood of 1981.*

At about this time Mr. Alec Brown installed the radiators and coupled the central heating to our existing school system. This again was a task that involved specialist knowledge and we are very grateful for Alec's hard work and expertise. Finally the floor screed was laid by John Marsh and the room decorated and the carpet tiles supplied by F.F. & F. of Highbridge.

Another document kept by the school is the School Log in which the headteacher notes items of interest on a day-to-day basis. This includes how the extremes of climate have affected the school. The following extracts refer to the drought of 1976 and the flood of 1981:

**1976**
**1 July**
Today some of Class 1 were taken to Minehead by myself (Mr Powell), Mrs Rogers and Mrs Logan. This visit included a trip on the Minehead/Blue Anchor steam railway followed by a swim in the outdoor pool. It was the hottest day on record!!
**3 July**
Today, Saturday, the fifth school fête held in our grounds. Many parents, friends and children attended and a record £224 was raised for our school funds.
**6 July**
This evening a Managers' meeting was held in the school. Managers were told of intended 'cuts' in educational spending.
**13 July**
We have today had problems with the school water supply. Water was cut off for a short period only but the quality of drinking water was very poor. There is now every effort being made in school for the conservation of water as we enter further into the period of prolonged drought!!
**16 July**
The end of the hottest and driest Summer Term on record according to all available statistics. At times the temperature in school has been unbearable but the teaching staff and in particular the Canteen staff, have coped magnificently. The school swimming pool at one period recorded 28 degrees C. The school swimming pool is to be kept open during the holidays – some parents have volunteered to operate a rota system of supervisors. A small charge is to be made for expenses incurred with chemicals, etc.

**1981**
**14 Dec ***
These floods were the result of very high winds, a blizzard and a high tide at Burnham-on-Sea. The Sea Wall caved in and the entire area around West Huntspill was affected by floods. Many people came to help with the damp and damaged school but I should like to record the more immediate help of my Staff who,

for a whole week, 'set to' with bucket and broom. Needless to say – the school was closed.

**1982**
**5 Jan**
Returned to school today after a damp, cold and very wintry Christmas break. The furniture and carpets are still in a turmoil and we have to wait patiently for new replacements in the way of books and carpets, etc. In all about £800 damage resulted from the floods.

* The extreme weather and floods occurred on Sunday 13 December through into the early hours of Monday 14 December.

The school continues to adapt and thrive. In the years following the Second World War it became a primary school only, pupils aged 11 and above moving on to the comprehensive school in Highbridge. In recent years a special-needs unit for Somerset has been established and at the time of writing has seven pupils. In 1998 the school celebrated its centenary.

# BALLIOL HALL

Since the establishment of the school in New Road in 1898 the old school buildings have been developed into the Sunday School and social centre of the village, providing the facilities of a village hall. The main expansion of facilities was made in 1936 when the Revd Hodge provided the southern extension which was named the Balliol Hall. The *Bridgwater Mercury* of 25 March 1936 reported:

*Monday was an outstanding day in the annals of West Huntspill. It marked the official opening of Balliol Hall, a building attached to the schoolroom for use as a young men's club. The building has only been made possible by the generosity of the Rector (Rev. R.C.V. Hodge) and Mrs Hodge, and it should provide a place where the parishioners can meet together for fellowship and recreation. The lofty building, which measures 45ft by 30ft, is afforded ample light in the daytime by large Crittall windows, and at night is electrically illuminated. Already one large billiard table and two smaller tables have been installed and the hall is amply equipped for amusement.*

Over the years since then various adaptations and extensions have been made, virtually all by voluntary fund-raising often through such bodies as the Harvest Supper Committee, the Balliol Hall Committee and grant funds from the Parish Council.

In 1976 the land adjacent to the Balliol Hall was purchased from the Church Commissioners to provide car parking. In 2001 a large extension to improve storage facilities was added and new

*The old schoolroom (built in 1828) on School Lane, 1999.*
*The Balliol Hall was built on to the 1876 school extension in 1936.*

*Balliol Hall and the church tower.*

windows installed with the aid of a grant from the Wyvern Trust which was obtained by the Chairman of the Balliol Short Mat Bowls Club, whose members use the building. Indeed, over the years many of the users of the hall, such as the WI, Drama Club, Keep Fit Club, Cub Pack and Horticultural Society, have made donations for hall improvements. Labour for redecoration of the building has also been provided on a voluntary basis. There are still plans for further expansion of the facilities. Being classed as a church hall the grants available for village halls are not available. Therefore the work done on and for the hall by the community over the generations is most notable.

The Harvest Supper Committee should be paid a special tribute for the help which it gave in making improvements to the hall possible. The committee was formed at the beginning of the 1960s and originated when Marie Gannicott, David Holley and John and Jenny Groves were visiting other Harvest Suppers and providing entertainment during the evening. Eventually, at Jenny's suggestion, a committee for West Huntspill was formed. Other people in the village were asked to help and the first supper, catering for 100 people, was held. After the first Harvest Supper all the profits were given to charities, but in subsequent years the money was kept to pay for the hire of tabling, seating, etc. It was also decided to plough the money back into a fund to improve the facilities at the Balliol Hall as up-to-date facilities were sadly lacking. Other events such as fêtes, whist drives, a knockout competition, carol singing, etc. were held towards this end.

The improvement of the premises began in 1968. The first project was building a new cloakroom, later to be followed by the building of the hydraulic stage in 1970. The kitchen was then updated, a central heating system installed and a much needed new toilet block built (in 1968) to replace the old outside toilets. Finally, the car park was provided. To enable all these projects to proceed, a loan was taken up with the bank whilst people in the village kindly provided interest-free loans. Many fund-raising events were held to pay back these funds. Improvements continued with the hall being brought up to fire-regulation standards, and new chairs, tabling and cupboards being provided. However, a lot of hard work by volunteers was needed to see the project through. Some old-fashioned bartering also took place. To pay the supplier for the hydraulic pump for the stage, a local builder promised to build him a new front window. A local farmer then offered to pay for the window if he could have the hard core that was being excavated from the site. So everyone was happy; the hydraulic stage proved to be a great success and is still in use today.

In 1971 a sub committee of the St Peter's Parochial Church Council was formed to run the hall and this continues today as the Balliol Hall Committee, albeit with some different members.

*Barbecue at Balliol Hall, 1997.*

## Playgroup

*West Huntspill Playgroup children and staff made a papier mâché caterpillar in 1978.*
*The colourful caterpillar was taken to the school and paraded around the playground.*
*The photo shows Mrs Yvette Haines, a Playgroup helper.*

*West Huntspill Playgroup's Christmas party at the Balliol Hall, 1987.*

*Chapter Six*

# PLAYGROUP

West Huntspill Playgroup was opened on Monday 13 September 1976 through the hard work of Diane Roper, Jenny Weeden and Monica Hall. Diane left the group in 1981 and Jenny in 1983, the running then continuing under the supervision of Monica Hall. In 1984 Carol Partridge joined the staff followed by Jean Worth in 1986 and Heather Kerr-Peterson in 1988. The latter four members of staff formed a very successful Playgroup team until Monica Hall retired in 2000 – a partnership of over 65 years! On Monica's retirement, Jean Worth took over as supervisor and the staff team was joined by Alison Jones.

For many years the group opened for three sessions a week but now an extra two sessions each week are held for the children who will start school the following September. Linked to the Under Fives Group is the Toddler Group which was formed in September 1984 and meets every Monday afternoon.

For 14 years the group was based in the Balliol Hall. This involved moving all of the equipment and hall furniture at the beginning and end of every session. When the LEA abolished school meals in April 1991 the school kitchen at West Huntspill school was no longer required for cooking school meals and as a consequence the canteen was freed up for other usage during the morning. Talks between the Headmaster, School Governors and Playgroup resulted in the move to the canteen the following September – in time for their 15th birthday.

The move to the canteen involved considerable work: the old kitchen equipment had to be removed, toilets installed and wash basins put in, etc. A local firm quoted £2500 for the job but obviously this was out of the question. Parents then rallied around and contributed their skills. A structural engineer, builders, a carpenter and joiner, bricklayers, and

*West Huntspill Playgroup's last session in the Balliol Hall, 1991.*

*West Huntspill Under Fives Group (Playgroup) – the 15th Anniversary celebrations in their new home at the school canteen, September 1991. West Huntspill children include: Thomas Roberts, Benjamin Higgs, Bethan Davies, Richard Lumley, Nathanial Bird, Sarah Swift, Sarah House, Matthew Counsell, Christopher Campbell, Robert Fisher, Amanda March.*

*West Huntspill Under Fives planting trees at the Ilex Play Area, January 1993. The adults are: Tracy Shaw, Carol Partridge, Heather Kerr-Peterson and Pauline House. The children are: Jonathon Shaw, Gemma King, Kevin Wakefield, Stacey Hannington, Jason Day, Sarah House, Sarah Brown and Alex Boyer.*

*West Huntspill Under Fives' Teddy Bears' Picnic in the school grounds, 1998.*

*West Huntspill Under Fives planting trees on Mrs Monica Hall's retirement, July 2000.*
The staff members are: *Carol Partridge, Heather Kerr-Peterson and Jean Worth.*

many more gave freely of their time in order to make the project viable. And there was plenty of unskilled voluntary help as well. In all, the conversion cost £750 on a DIY basis and the money was raised in four months – quite an achievement. The move was first suggested in April 1991 and the group had moved into the school canteen by the following September. (A great deal was learnt about building regulations and the different LEA departments!)

Over the years the Playgroup has always been extremely lucky with very supportive helpers and parents. What would they have done without the parents who have made and mended, donated and decorated, and encouraged all of their efforts? In 1995 when the Pre-school Playgroup Association changed its name to the Pre-school Learning Alliance, the Playgroup changed its name to West Huntspill School Under Fives Group. This represents their close links with the school and their commit-ment to under fives' education.

They have been lucky enough to be able to use the school playground, garden and swimming pool; whilst the most recent shared facility with the reception class is an enclosed play area with a lovely playhouse.

Down through the years many children living in West Huntspill and the surrounding area have passed through the group and their most recent claim to fame is Lee Childs from Pawlett who was a previous Playgroup child. Lee is now a professional tennis player having just played and won his first match for England in the Davis Cup against Portugal. Monica Hall well remembers clambering onto the flat roof at the Balliol Hall to retrieve the many footballs kicked there by Lee! It is always rewarding and fun working with children; in what other job can you happily be a slithering snake, make monstrous creations or escape to the land of make believe? The Playgroup could easily write their own book about the children's sayings, if only they had been jotted down! What about the three-year-old boy standing in the 'home corner' saying 'beep, beep, beep, beep, beep'? When asked what he was, he replied, 'I'm making toast and that's the smoke alarm'!

Over the years the group has been visited by lambs, tortoises, a tarantula, the police and many other visitors. A very special visitor dressed in red always comes to the group's Christmas party; John Joyce has never let them down! They have visited the library, the fire station, the steam trains at the Playing Field, Secret World and indoor activity centres at Cheddar and Weston-super-Mare. The latter is really very exciting for the children. For many the highlight is the coach ride, especially for those who have never been on a coach before. Another highlight of the year is the annual Teddy Bears' Picnic in the school garden. The children make their own picnic, which is great fun even if some of the bread does get eaten before it has a chance to be made into a sandwich. And the group has also taken part in local community events. Every year they enjoy making an exhibition of work for the local WI Spring Show. Children particularly enjoyed helping to plant trees at the Ilex Play Area when it was being landscaped.

In 1996 the group provided a display of work and made a model of St Peter's and All Hallows Church for St Peter's Flower Festival. As part of the Methodist Church celebrations and festival of 1993 they tried their hands at weaving and flower arranging.

The children have even been recorded for posterity in the village time capsule. A photo of the 'leavers' group of 1999 as well as some pieces of the children's work were included in the capsule which celebrated the millennium. At the time of writing, their next milestone is their 25th anniversary in September 2001 which is eagerly awaited.

## Chapter Seven

# ANCIENT PROPERTIES

## SEALEY'S FARM, WEST HUNTSPILL

In 1999 a survey of Sealey's Farmhouse was carried out by a member of the Somerset Vernacular Research Group. It was decided that the land on which Sealey's Farm, as it is now known, was originally founded, probably belonged to the Sydenham family of East Bridgwater. A century after the Domesday Book Robert de Sydenham took over the manor known as Sideba (meaning place beside a home). The Sydenhams flourished, and remained in East Bridgwater until 1450 when they moved to Combe Sydenham near the Quantock Hills.

A tenant or yeoman farmer would have been put in charge of the original farm, and the farm maintained by the Sydenham landlords. The success of the farm ensured its maintenance and survival to this day. Metre-thick cob walls, and the line and shape of the present building, indicate that the farmhouse was almost certainly a one-storey hall house with a thatched roof, central fireplace, and a cross passage dividing the house in two.

In the 17th century the south end of the building was extended and built upwards with a gable, using squared Ham stone. The cob walls were extended upwards to match the new south end. Well-built stone fireplaces with spiral staircases beside them were built at the north and south ends of the house and the north fireplace incorporates a curing chamber. At this stage the new roof would have been thatch as it had been

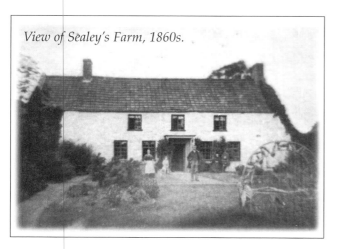

*View of Sealey's Farm, 1860s.*

before. At a later date still an extension kitchen was built at the north end using 9-inch brick, and including another large fireplace with a bread oven and an iron door. The cross passage still existed, and the front of the house faced east. In the 20th century, when the old farmhouse was renovated and saved from dereliction, the west-facing back of the longhouse was transformed into the house front. There are many interesting features still to be seen, among them a cruck beam which definitely dates back to the early-15th century, remains of a spice cupboard and blue lias flagstones in the extended north end of the house. There are also fire-blackened stones in remains of the curing chamber, together with rough-hewn timbers both there and in part of the north stone spiral staircase. This staircase is still in use.

A survey carried out at the Somerset Archivist Office showed that in 1840 the old holding was known as Palmer's Farm and consisted of 160 acres. The landowner was John Sealey and the occupier William Norris. The rent per annum was 3s.4d. In 1841 William Norris was aged 30, his wife Jane was 20 and they had a daughter, Mary, of 11 months. Also living in the house was the family servant Betsy Cousins, aged 35, and a manservant by the name of William Milton, aged 15.

By 1851 the name of the house had been changed to White Castle. As yet there is no clue about this change. It is remotely possible that the house was in some way connected with the salt trade as many properties involved in this trade had 'white' added to their name. By this time the Norris family had four children, a dairymaid and a general servant. The year 1861 saw six children in the family and the land had by this time been increased to 182 acres. There is evidence of only one servant, a dairymaid. It is likely that the older children – aged 20, 18, 16 and 14 years – were by now helping on the farm. In 1871 William was 63 years old and Jane 53. The two youngest children, James (18) and Thomas (15) were still at home. There was one dairymaid and one general servant. By the time of the 1881 Census the son James had taken over the farm, and by 1891 the wife Jane Norris had become a widow. She was fairly 'well-to-do' and was able to live 'on her own means'. The youngest son Thomas became a coal merchant branching out into different fields of industry, a transition made possible by the new railways.

## Sealey's Farm

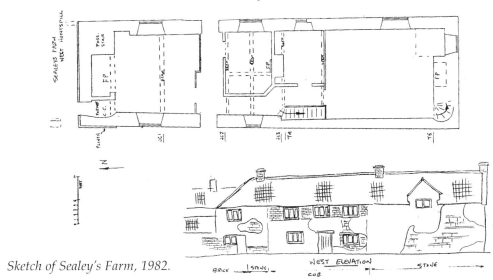

*Sketch of Sealey's Farm, 1982.*

*Restoration of Sealey's Farm, mid 1980s.*

*Sealey's Farm, 1999.*

Since that time the building and land have been known as Sealey's Farm after the two landowning brothers Sealey. It remained a working farm until the mid-20th century, and then the land was sold. After a succession of owners the house became neglected until the building became ruinous before being saved and restored in the 1980s. At this juncture the roof was tiled. A survey carried out under the auspices of the District Council in 1982 led to the farmhouse being designated a Grade II listed building because of its historical interest and value. The following is a survey report made when the house stood derelict:

## SEDGEMOOR DISTRICT
*Huntspill Sealey's Farm, West Huntspill.*
*ST 308 454    2/4    Grade III*

*This large farmhouse in the village of West Huntspill is at present empty and somewhat neglected, rendering has fallen from the East side exposing the wall construction, the West side is almost inaccessible due to the overgrown trees and bushes of the former garden.*

*The wall construction is cob, brick, and stone, the windows mostly recent, the roof of triple roll tiles. The South end of the house has a hamstone coping, also coped are the front and rear gables at the South end, now with windows lighting only the first floor but the former stair at the South end indicates that there was an attic, presumably lit by windows in the gables. At the North end the house has been extended, the extension walls being 9" brick, this extension housing a large fireplace and an oven with an iron door and clearly added as a kitchen. Beyond this room is a narrow store room and a lean-to to the West.*

*The exposed wall construction of the West side shows that the earliest part was a low cob house with at its North end a veil built stone fireplace with a distinct plinth course some 2' above ground level, this fireplace may however have been added to the cob house. The South end is much higher and well built in squared lias. At a later period the low cob walls were extended upwards in brick to the same level as the stone part. Also extended upwards was the stone fireplace block, later the North extensions were made.*

*The approx. 4' raising of the cob house is in brick of quite even texture and is probably of 18 Century date and consists of courses of headers separated by single courses of stretchers (although in places this single row of stretchers becomes two or even three rows), that is, English bond. The North extension to the house is as far as can be seen evenly bonded, five courses of stretchers to each row of headers English garden wall bond.*

*Ignoring the added North kitchen, the first room is entered beside the fireplace. Much detail is obscured but the fireplace is large, the lintel is hidden but can be seen over the entry where it is clearly sooted and it is almost*

*certain that this entry is through a former curing chamber. The masonry block on the other side of the fireplace is of uncertain purpose but the front appears to be false and it sounds as if there is a space behind it, in the room above, the wall is rather curved and this may have been a stair. The one beam is plastered.*

*The cross passage partitions have both been rebuilt, beyond the cross passage a lateral passage has been made by narrowing the next room, here can be seen the remains of a four-panelled framed ceiling, plain chamfered. The small fireplace is an insertion. At the end of this room there is a step in the West wall where the stone building starts, the parts so far described are in the cob walled part. A stair has been built against the West wall, across the passage from it is a room only about 8' wide with a half beam at each end with rounded step and runout stops to the chamfer.*

*The South end room is large and has at its South end a blocked fireplace and a ruinous stair rising over it.*

*On the first floor is little detail of note but the roof structure may be seen in part. The roof of the South end has been replaced but under paper and plaster can be seen the remains of two trusses, one at the fireplace front and one at the end of the stone building in line with the foot of the stair, little can be seen of these trusses but they appear to have heavy principal rafters with a collar.*

*On the other side of the partition in which the second of these trusses (T4) is buried is a further truss, by comparison with those to the North a jointed cruck (JC3) but obscured. JC1 and JC2 are clearly jointed crucks although papered over, these have a trenched purlin at the wall top and one higher under the ceiling with perhaps another even higher up in the inaccessible area above the ceiling. The wall top curves in at the cruck joint and leaves a wall thickness of only a foot or so at the former eaves. It is not possible to precisely date the earliest cob house, it may be an open Hall house of the medieval period and its former height would lend credence to this view, its construction, cob and jointed cruck, is a common medieval form but it is also possible that the building dates from the 16 Century. There are too few dating clues to be sure.*
**R.G. Gilson, March 1982.**

# Nos 5–7 Silver Street

The following is the report of a survey made in 1990 of one of the buildings in Silver Street:

## SEDGEMOOR DISTRICT
*Huntspill 5/7 Silver Street.*
*ST 305 456*

*In the centre of the village near the church, this former farmhouse has been divided into two dwellings.*

The walls are of coursed stone, the roof tiled. Further buildings have been added at each end, the front has been altered to incorporate two doorways, the back has an added lean-to. Most windows are relatively recent but there is still one stone mullioned front window of four lights, the moulding somewhat cleaned up but originally hollow chamfered. This window is of hamstone and of the same material are two former kneelers for vanished copings, now well down in the front wall below a clear raised area.

Internally the layout has been somewhat altered by conversion into two dwellings but the original plan can still be seen. At the East end is the former kitchen, the large fireplace with a former curing chamber to one side and perhaps an oven to the other.

The central area was probably built as an unheated entry/stair room. Now a separate dwelling, the West room was the Parlour with the four light window, a stair now inserted in the back corner.

Several beams are visible, all have scroll stops.

Parts of four roof trusses are visible, altered, the roof raised. These trusses have or had dovetailed halving jointed collars.

The beams, roof details, and plan, all indicate a house of mid 17 Century date, without doubt a farmhouse. The use of hamstone for windows and other architectural details is surprising at such a distance from the quarry, although the house is modest this does indicate willingness (and ability) to spend a considerable sum on its construction.

**R.G. Gilson, June 1990.**

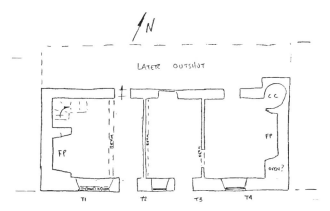

Sketch of 5–7 Silver Street.

Silver Street, late 1920s.

## Chapter Eight

# CLUBS, GROUPS & SOCIETIES

## BALLIOL SHORT-MAT BOWLING CLUB

Early in 1999, enthusiastic short-mat bowler Vincent Derham decided that it would be beneficial for the village to form its own bowling club, using the facilities at the Balliol Hall. To this end he tried to obtain funding from the National Lottery through Help The Aged Charity in order to form a Short-Mat Bowling Club for the Huntspills. An application was made and eventually a grant of £4640 from the lottery was awarded to enable the formation of the club and for equipment to be purchased. For this work Vincent was granted lifetime membership of the Millennium Awards Fellowship by the Millennium Awards Commission in February 2001.

An inaugural meeting of the Short-Mat Bowling Club was held on 1 September 1999 and 30 members from the villages of West and East Huntspill were enrolled. Vincent Derham was elected Chairman, Sarah Feltham Secretary, and Janet Loney Treasurer, together with five other members to form the committee. The club meets three times weekly for three-hour sessions which gives time for two games of bowls and a break for tea and a chat. After some 18 months the club has proved to be an outstanding success and continues to flourish socially and financially.

Although novices in the early days, members have proved worthy opponents at meetings with other clubs locally and have had many successes. Weekend trips are now being arranged. Recently a grant of £15000 was obtained from the Wyvern Trust to enable storage space to be created to store the club's equipment and that of other users of the Balliol Hall.

From little acorns big trees grow. A club has been formed that gives a great deal of pleasure to local people and the hall has benefited. Many people have derived happy hours in the company of other local residents and made new friends.

*Balliol Short-Mat Bowling Club, June 2001.*
*Vincent Derham takes careful aim.*

*Balliol Short-Mat Bowling Club, June 2001.*
*Janet Lockyer is on left discussing the winning shot with Mercy Twiner.*

# HUNTSPILL & DISTRICT CRICKET CLUB

There has been a cricket team in West Huntspill for over 100 years with only short breaks during the First and Second World Wars. During the early years the club played on any suitable farmer's field before setting up home at Grove Farm courtesy of Mr and Mrs W. Palmer in 1920. After several years of playing on any cut, flat strip of field, a proper square was laid which became one of the best in the area, the club playing against teams the length and breadth of the county. During these years the players were captained by Jack Baker and later by Gerry Roberts, and when the club reformed after the Second World War in 1946 the captaincy was held by Jim Coombes who continued in the post until 1963 when John Holley took over until 1971. John is one of the most prolific cricketers in the club's history, his bowling being much feared by opposing teams. He continued to play for the club until he moved away in the late 1970s.

In 1965 the club moved to its current home at the Memorial Ground Playing Fields in New Road, where the Parish Council purposely laid a square. The club can boast being the only club in the league with a 'road' passing through its outfield. A pavilion was built by the members and in April 1967 the Club Chairman Mr H.L. Sheperd invited Mr F.C. Edwards (Chairman of the Bridgwater Rural District Council) to open the pavilion. A match against a celebrity XI was played to celebrate this opening. Some of the visiting players included Bill Andrews, Brian Lobb and Harold Gimmlett of Somerset County Cricket Club.

In 1968 Huntspill became one of the co-founders of the Highbridge and District Midweek League (now known as the *Bridgwater Mercury* Wednesday League). The club played in this league until the mid 1980s, through the years winning the league and knockout cup on numerous occasions. Captains of this XI have included Winston Hand, John Smith, Mike Hawkings, Stephen Pegler, Colin Hand, Pete Hand, Andy Jarvis and John Jarvis.

In 1978 Huntspill & District played host to Somerset County Cricket Club for a testimonial match for their wicket keeper Derek Taylor, who at the time lived in Burnham-on-Sea. This evening match drew a large crowd to watch their local side play Viv Richards, Peter Denning, Mervyn Kitchen and co. The many hoping to see Viv Richards hitting the Huntspill bowlers to the surrounding fields were sadly disappointed when this great player was bowled out cheaply by Tony Penwill. However, he did make someone very happy because during the match he broke his bat and allowed it to be raffled off, leaving one lucky fan with a unique souvenir of the evening! The club's 1st XI joined Division 5 of the Somerset Cricket League in 1978 and were promoted in 1979, 1983 and 1984. The 2nd XI joined the league in 1985. Over the years Dave Counsell has proved to be a high wicket taker for the club, appearing in the division best averages many times up to and including the year 2001. Since joining the club he has taken over 900 league wickets including a haul of 10–24 against Huish and Langport in 1983. Between 1980 and 1991 Andrew Jarvis proved to be a very fine batsman for the club scoring 5597 runs and topping the league division average in 1987 by scoring 1073 runs. Colin Hand captained the club on and off from the early 1970s to the early 1990s. He was a well respected all-rounder; a right-handed batsman, left-handed bowler and a superb slip fielder. The club continues to play in this league with its 1st XI currently playing in Division 6.

In the late 1970s John Davey saw the need to encourage young people to play cricket and formed a youth XI which he entered in the Taunton and District Youth League. In 1979 initially there was just one under-16s team with 11 boys aged 11 upwards playing in it. Over the last 20 years John has developed this one team into a thriving youth section which currently runs four league teams at under-11 and two at under-13, as well as an under-15 team and an under-9 team which plays friendly matches. Since the early 1980s Huntspill's under-13s have taken a least one team to the Kilve Under-13 Festival. The club always enjoys the day out to Kilve Beach and has returned with the Jack Hancock Trophy and Man of the Match Awards many times. In 1981 the club youth team made the national newspapers when they bowled out Brymore School for 0 runs. The bowlers in this game were Chris Derham, Steve Hicks, Paul Tippetts and Paul Maxwell, and the wicket keeper was Philip Davey. In 1990 under the captaincy of Lee Saunders, the under-15 team were Champions of Somerset in the Sun Life of Canada Cup and represented the county in the regional finals. Most recently in 1999 the under-11 side won the Taunton & District League Plate Competition under the captaincy of Matthew Counsell.

As well as Huntspill there are many local sides who have players whose love of the game began in the Huntspill youth sides, notably Darren Read, Stuart Standerwick, Lee Trumper and Andy Wood who play for Bridgwater, and Chris Gange who is currently in the Somerset County Cricket Academy.

The most recent highlight in the club's history was Huntspill's 'day out' to play on the County Ground in Taunton. The club made it to the finals in the Somerset Cricket Association Junior Knockout Cup. Having beaten the opposition of Crewkerne, Weston-super-Mare and Chilton Crickets, the club played Castle Cary in the final. Huntspill sadly lost in this match but the opportunity of playing on the County Ground will live with the members for many years to come.

In 2000, thanks to the hard work of Sally March, the club received a grant for Wyvern Waste to install a non-turf artificial wicket. The continued support given to the club by the Parish Council allows it to develop and thrive and look forward to the next 100 years of cricket in West Huntspill.

# Cricket Club

*Highbridge, Huntspill and District Cricket Club, c.1900.*

*Huntspill and District Cricket Club, 1965. Left to right, back: Bill Plews, Stephen Pegler, Mike Hawkings, Alan Dyer, John Holley, Michael Cavill, Patrick Doble, Cyril Hawkins, Arthur Holley; front: Lenny Psyk, George Perry, Ken Dyer.*

*Huntspill and District Cricket Club, mid 1970s. Left to right, back: Tony Penwill, George Perry, Brian Purnell, Pete Bamber, Gerald Pople, John Holley, Cyril Hawkins, Stephen Pegler; front: Colin Hand, John Smith, Mike Hawkings, John Davey.*

*Huntspill and District Cricket Club, SCA Minor KO Cup Runners-up, 1991, at Somerset County Ground Taunton. Left to right, back: Amanda Counsell (scorer), Dave Counsell, Mark Doble, Dave Amesbury, Colin Hand, Pete Hand, Matthew Crook; front: John Doble, Lee Saunders, Philip Coggins (Capt.), Kevin Perrett, Simon Doble, Andrew Jarvis.*

# WEST HUNTSPILL TABLE TENNIS CLUB

*by Pete Bamber*

West Huntspill Table Tennis Club was started after my passion for table tennis was passed on to my children. When my daughter reached the age of nine she was tall enough, so I took her into the Bridgwater training facility at Chilton School. Although she was taught the basics, there were too many youngsters there for her to progress as fast as I would have liked and unless she showed exceptional talent she would not get the 'one-to-one' coaching available. I thought that there was a better way in so much that any child, no matter how good or bad, could learn and enjoy the game. My skills at coaching were non existent since I was playing Bridgwater Premier Division standard league table tennis, but my enthusiasm to put something back into the game spurred me on to call a meeting on 20 September 1978 to see if there was any interest among the villagers of West Huntspill to start a club at the Balliol Hall.

The response was more than I had hoped for and a night was set to call a second meeting to discuss how we would run it and where we would get the equipment from. No grants were available since the majority of the members were adults, so a membership fee was discussed with a view to buying a table and paying for the hire of the hall. This worked well and soon we had enough for our first table. It was not brilliant but it was flat, the right colour and had its own legs. The problem was that the club became so popular that we were in danger of losing members because we did not have enough tables. There were more and more children turning up each week and I decided to divide the club into two sessions, early evening for kids and after 8p.m. for adults. The extra numbers brought in much-needed revenue to enable us to buy another table. And so it progressed until we had five tables and a reasonable standard of ping pong going on.

I realised then that if we were to be successful the future of the club lay in the hands of the young-sters and their ability to improve at league standard. To this end I enrolled on the English Table Tennis Coaching system and achieved the Club Coach Certificate at a weekend assessment at Locking Air Base. Revitalised, I entered all of the youngsters in the Somerset Knockout Competition and to my surprise they all did very well, winning a number of rounds. In the early 1980s two men, Kevin Hood from Reading and John Neale from Birmingham, joined the club and shared my view of the way forward. The three of us played at a reasonable standard and it was suggested that we each took charge of a side to encourage three youngsters each in a team. Since the kids were at an age where they

could not drive, it worked perfectly for the transport to away matches. The years have now rolled by and the kids (all grown up and married, some with kids) drive me and Kevin to away matches because they think the stress might wear us out before the match!

The membership has dropped somewhat with other hobbies and pastimes having become available, but the club is in a healthy position. The fund-raising that enables us to continue, in the early days Race Nights and the legendary Grand National Jumble Sale, has been replaced in recent years by a Lottery Bonus Ball Bonanza. Players have come and gone and come back again, but some have remained, people like Mike Fear, my son Simon, and Kevin Hood who for nearly 15 years have been the backbone of the club. A regular membership of about 20 continues to ensure that West Huntspill Table Tennis Club survives. The standard is such that we now boast two teams in the Bridgwater Premier Division, so I am back where I started!

# WEST HUNTSPILL HARVEST HOME & FLOWER SHOW

West Huntspill Harvest Home and Flower Show ran from the 1930s until 1940 when the Second World War intervened. It was held in a field opposite Greenwood Farm (now Greenwood Lodge) and there was a procession to the field after a service in the Parish Church. Lunch was then served and in the afternoon sports were followed by tea and a dance in the evening. In 1938 the officers of the committee were: Chairman: Mr Reg Clark of Greenwood Farm; Secretary: Mr Archie Dean, Church Road; Treasurer: Mr Cox of Westminster Bank, Highbridge. That same year, 1938, Victor Dyer of Central Press in Highbridge printed 500 service papers for the Harvest Home Thanksgiving Service at a cost of £2.10s.0d. The size and popularity of the Harvest Home can be judged by the amount of food ordered for the teas, as recorded in the minutes of a Ladies' Committee meeting. This included: three hams from Highbridge Bacon Co., ten gallons of milk from Highbridge Creamery, 5lbs of tea from the Post Office, 24lbs of lump sugar from Miss Nutt and 35qt bread. Apparently Mr Gulliford's cake was so good in 1938 that it was decided to order the same again in 1939. This comprised 28lbs of seed cake, 137lbs of fruit cake and 36lbs of Madeira cake. For this inordi-nately large supply of cake Mr Gulliford of Church Street, Highbridge, charged £5.16s.8d. The ladies hired table linen, crockery and cutlery from Bird & Sons of Winscombe, but they were also charged for breakages: namely 1s.0d. for a milk jug.

Side shows provided added entertainment, these being supplied by John Cole of Staple Hill, Bristol. A letter from Mr Cole states:

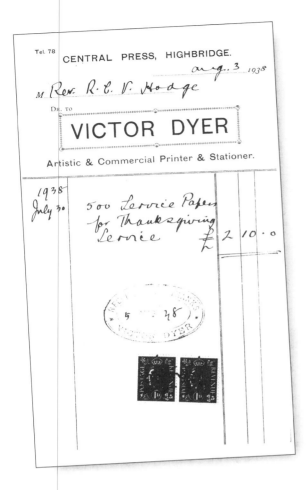

*Harvest Home bill for printing, 1938.*

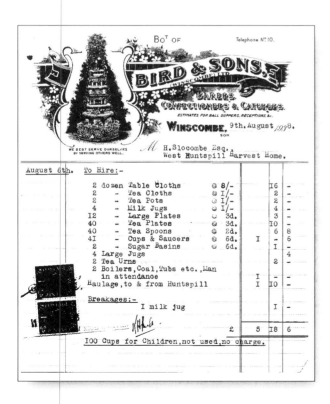

*Harvest Home bill for hiring crockery, etc., 1938.*

*I the undersigned agree to provide amusements for the West Huntspill Harvest Home and Flower Show to be held on Aug 12 1939 and also pay £6.0.0. for same and hoping to be favoured with a fine day.*

Miss Nutt, who owned a shop on the site of the present Sundowner Hotel, was 'anxious to know if any sanitary arrangements were being made for show people as previously they have been a nuisance to her.' The marquees, tabling and seating in 1939 were hired from Locker & Co. of East Huntspill at a cost of £14.14s.0d. The same year six wooden spoons at a cost of 2s.6d. and six china eggs at a cost of 6d. were purchased from John Tyler (Highbridge) Ltd for the sports.

Interestingly, a letter dated 30 January 1939 from Mrs J.B. Hodge of Huntspill Rectory to Mr Archie Dean, thanks the Harvest Home Committee for the sum of £3.16s.2d. This was a donation made towards the Huntspill Nursing Association. At that time nurses were paid for by the villagers; as indicated in the article on the Welfare Clinic in the opening chapter of this volume.

Sadly the Harvest Home did not make a comeback after the war and only the Flower Show survives from the pre-war Harvest Home event.

# THE FLOWER SHOW
## (LATER THE HORTICULTURAL SOCIETY)

The first Flower Show was held in 1939, a draft schedule for which event lists a total of 42 classes. The grand sum of £11.8s.0d. was allocated for prize money, printing costs were estimated to be in the region of £4 or £5, and with an anticipated receipt of £1.10s.0d. for entry fees, the committee looked set to be within their budget of £15. The vegetable and fruit classes are very similar to today's events. The flower classes were more limited; although there was a class for a specimen fern or an aspidistra. There was a choice of six classes in the ladies' section. These included: an arrangement of flowers; pot of jam; fruit cake not to have cost more than 3s.0d.; a dish of best cooked potatoes; one dozen hen's eggs, white; and one dozen hen's eggs, brown. There was also a children's section with a wild-flower and grass-arrangement class. There were two age groups for the children – under tens and over tens.

The rules of the show seem to have remained the same with very few exceptions. One interesting rule which acted as a warning for any over-zealous gardener, was that: 'the committee shall have the right without previous notice, to visit the garden or allotment of any intending exhibitor to inspect the crops there growing.' There is no record of whether or not this rule was put into effect! There was, though, the expulsion of an exhibitor in the times of the late Mr

## The Flower Show

*Flower Show martial arts demonstration, 1987.*

*Bridgwater Kestrels Marching Band
at a Flower Show, date unknown.*

*Flower Show field with the tea tent, Balliol Hall
and St Peter's Church in background, 1987.*

*The judges' and officials' luncheon, Flower Show, 1987.
Bill Fisher is standing and Audrey Young is seated in
the foreground. Seated in the background are Vi Holley
and Jean Davis, who were responsible for the lunches.
Charles Langdon is seated next to Audrey Young.*

*Flower Show exhibits.*

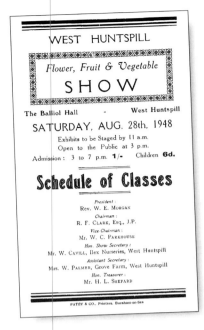

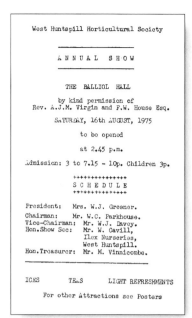

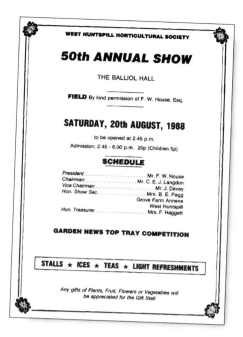

Above left: *West Huntspill Flower, Fruit and Vegetable Show, 1948. This was the first show held after the Second World War.*
Middle: *Horticultural Society Annual Show programme, 16 August 1975. This was the Society's first show at the Balliol Hall.*
Right: *Horticultural Society 50th Annual Show programme, 20 August 1988.*

Wesley Cavill. A gentleman kept winning all of the fruit classes but suspicions were not aroused until the committee added the class 'Any Other Fruit', whereupon the gentleman in question entered a honeydew melon, from which the label had quite clearly been removed. Enquiries were made and it was discovered that there were no fruit trees in the exhibitor's garden. Apparently it was also a known fact that the gentleman visited the greengrocers in Highbridge and carefully selected his fruit from those shops. Naturally he was asked not to enter the show again! Perhaps a modern-day equivalent of the above rule should be introduced!

The first available minute-book for the Flower Show dating from after the Second World War is from 1948. The minutes were for a meeting of 'Flower Show Section of Harvest Home Committee' which was held in the Methodist Schoolroom on Thursday 29 July 1948. The following officers were elected: President: Revd W.E. Morgan; Chairman: Mr R.F. Clark; Vice Chairman: Mr W.C. Parkhouse; Treasurer: Mr H.L. Sheperd; Hon. Sec. Mr W. Cavill; Assistant Hon. Sec.: Mrs W. Palmer. The other committee members present were: Mesdames Sheperd, Hancock and Welch, and Messrs D. Hancock, L.A. Davey, E.J. Edwards and A.K.M. Shattock. The first minute states: 'It was resolved to hold a Flower Show this year.' The second minute is really the start of the Flower Show as we know it today and indicates why the Harvest Home possibly did not recover after the war:

*Resolved to function henceforth purely as a Flower Show committee leaving the Harvest Home to be revised at a later date as and when food supplies etc. become easier. The hope was expressed that another year a fête might be incorporated with the flower show providing a source of income and making a wider appeal to the village.*

The show was to be held on Saturday 28 August 1948 at the Balliol Hall and was to be opened at 3.00p.m. by the Mayor of Bridgwater.

The 1948 show appears to have been very successful with a high number of exhibits and a profit of £9.16s.ld. The following year the committee decided to affiliate the show to the Royal Horticultural Society and to apply for a Banksian Medal Award. This award was given to the exhibitor with the highest amount of prize money. At this juncture, the show also moved to the New Dining Hall (the present canteen) and classroom on the school site where, it was felt, 'the position would be advantageous'.

In January 1952 the committee decided on the formation of a society, the name of which was to be the West Huntspill Flower, Fruit and Vegetable Society, with the promotion of the cultivation of flowers, fruit and vegetables as its aim. The rules of the society were drawn up and passed unanimously. The following meeting in March 1952 minuted that the name be amended and changed to the West Huntspill Horticultural Society. In 1949 Mr W.C. Parkhouse was elected Chairman, a position he then held until his death in 1976. During those 27 years he never missed a meeting.

There are many people in the village who have worked hard and tirelessly on behalf of the Flower Show and it would be difficult to mention them all

## *The Flower Show*

*Flower Show fancy-dress competition at Chestnut Field, 1953. Children present include: Michael Watts and Alan Jones.*

*Flower Show fancy-dress competition at Chestnut Field, August 1957.*

*West Huntspill Flower Show, mid 1950s. Fancy-dress entrants and friends. The adults are: George and Annie Haggett, Mrs Comer, Shirley Viner and Mr Stephens; the children are: Barbara Haggett, with basket, and Alan Jones, as a policeman.*

*West Huntspill Flower Show, August 1974. Prize-winners of the fancy dress. The children in the picture include Paul Derham and Stephen Hall. This was the last year that the show was held at Chestnut Field.*

*Horticultural Society Show, 1980s. Fred House, President, admires a floral exhibit with two young entrants.*

here. Past Presidents and Chairmen include Mr Reg Clark, Mrs W.J. Greener, Mr Wesley Cavill, Mr John Davey, Mr Ernie Gillard and Mr Charles Langdon. Mr Wesley Cavill was the first Secretary of the Show and was later Chairman for many years. He was also a well-known judge at local shows and continued to be a lifelong supporter of the event. At the time of writing, the current Chairman and President are Mr Bill Fisher and Mr Fred House who have both been associated with the event since the 1950s.

The Committee held a few spring Shows after 1950 but these seem to have been abandoned for various reasons after 1954. The venue for the Summer Show continued to be at the school until 1952 when Rookery Field opposite Greenwood Farm was used by kind permission of Mr and Mrs Greener. In 1953 the venue moved to Chestnut Field and stayed there until its final move to the Balliol Hall in 1975. This move was precipitated by the local vandals causing damage to the marquees and also by interference with the exhibits overnight; namely taking bites out of the fruit! Over the years cream teas, sports and children's fancy dress have remained integral features of the Show. For many years a dance was held after the close of the Show on the Saturday evening. Children taking part in the fancy dress would parade in their costumes. When the Show was held at the school the children would process from Court Farm drive to the school.

Many well-known local personalities and indeed some television celebrities have been asked to open the event and judge the fancy dress. These include Ken Rees, Richard Wyatt and Sheila Burnett. At the Show there have always been various side shows and stalls run by other village organisations. Entertainments have been provided by the Burtle Silver Band and majorettes. Various original competitions and prizes have attracted participants on Show days – among them tossing the sheaf, guessing the weight of pigs, lambs (and one year a goose which was then used as the prize for the skittle competition). The latter always attracted a great deal of attention with prizes such as a cockerel, a pig and even a leg of lamb for the gentleman winner and a shoulder of lamb for the lady winner.

Raising funds for the Show has always been a necessity and fund-raising efforts such as whist drives, dances, concerts and skittle weeks organised by Bill Fisher at the Artillery Arms have been popular. For the last few years the Horticultural Society has held a very successful plant sale in May. The Society celebrated holding its 50th Show in 1988, the President at that time being Mr Fred House, the Chairman Mr Charles Langdon and the Secretary Mrs Barbara Pegg.

In the year 2000, there were 130 classes at the Show, with a total of 577 exhibits from 82 entrants winning £245 in prize money. The fancy dress is still held and run by Mrs Betty Lambert. We now have a car-boot sale, which together with cream teas and stalls, including cakes and ice-creams, enabled the Show to make a profit of £289.57. The year 2000 Show Committee included Mr F. House as President; Mr R.W. Fisher as Chairman; Mr M. Watts as Vice-Chairman; Mrs J. Moreton as Secretary and Mrs K. Haggett as Treasurer. Other Committee members were Mrs M. House, Mr J. Davey, Mr and Mrs C. Langdon, Mrs Mary Watts, Mrs J. O'Neill, Mrs C. Hester and Mr L. Roper. It is hoped that this is one village tradition which will continue to flourish with the help of a great deal of support in the 21st century.

# THE WEST HUNTSPILL PLAYERS

Prebendary Morgan, the Rector of Huntspill, started the original West Huntspill Drama Club in 1950. Classes were run by the Bridgwater Technical College, the tutors being Mr Robert Parnell and Mrs Burston. When the classes finished Mr Maurice Vinnecombe of Alstone Road continued as the producer for the group. After Mr Vinnecombe left the group, there was a lapse until 1972 when the new West Huntspill Players were formed and performed their first production in 1973. For their first effort in the spring of that year they produced three one-act plays: *Maria Marten*, *The Bathroom Door* and *Brooch for the Bride*. The producer was Marie Gannicott with Reg Pike in charge of the scenery. Over the years Reg has built some stunning sets incorporating some very clever design work and revealing more than a smattering of artistic talent. Marie Gannicott continued as the producer and mainstay of the club for many years with a great number of production successes. When ill health sadly forced her retirement, Burt Jenkins continued as the producer, again with many successful productions.

For many years the club entered the *Evening Post* Rose Bowl Awards. The first award given to a member of the Club was to Mark Berry for Best Supporting Actor in *Diplomatic Baggage* by John Chapman. Later Burt Jenkins went on to win the Phöebe Rees Award for Best Supporting Actor in *When We Are Married* by J.B. Priestley. Although no other awards have come the club's way, the Players' productions are very popular in the village and are always sold out.

The group produces two three-act plays every year, one in April and one in October. Notable productions have included *Scrooge*, *The Ghost Train*, *Sailor Beware* and *Dry Rot*. The club also put on evenings of entertainment and revues in aid of different charities or for other fund-raising events. The original West Huntspill Players founder members from 1972 who are still very active in the club include David Holley, Reg Pike, Esme Gilling (née Wills) and Freda Richardson. Freda and David were associated with the original Drama Group in 1950. David has also been Chairman of the Players for many years.

## *The West Huntspill Players*

*West Huntspill Players*, Maria Marten, *1973.*
Left to right, standing: *Ken Davis, Reg Pike, Betty Darke,*
*Dorothy Mitchell, John Holley, Esme Wills, Betty Lambert,*
*John Mitchell, David Holley; seated: Mary Gillard,*
*June Holley, Judith Virgin, Jane Lambert and Pam Wills.*

*West Huntspill Players*, Look Out For The Catch
*by Jean McConnell, April 1978.*
Left to right: *Esme Wills, Mavourneen Orchard,*
*John Mitchell and Ken Davis.*

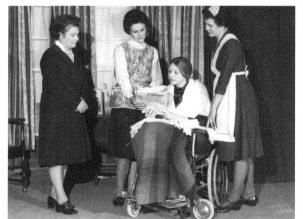

Left: *West Huntspill Players*, Brooch For The Bride,
*1973.* Left to right: *Freda Richardson, Pam Duffin,*
*Angela Darke, Monica Hall.*

Below: *West Huntspill Players. The present club was*
*formed in 1973. Pictured here is their production of* Dry
Rot *in April 1991. Left to right, back: Vour Orchard,*
*Stuart Golledge, Janet Holderness, Alan Jarvis, Mark*
*Berry, David Holley; front: Jonathan Cotton, Julie*
*Williams (née Doble), Burt Jenkins and Mandy Hayes.*

## The West Huntspill Players

**THE WEST HUNTSPILL PLAYERS**

*present*

# LOOK OUT
## FOR
# THE CATCH

*A Comedy by*
*JEAN McCONNELL*

27th, 28th & 29th April, 1978

Price 5p.

**THE WEST HUNTSPILL PLAYERS**

*present*

# 'FAREWELL, FAREWELL, EUGENE'

by John Vari
adapted by Rodney Ackland

25th, 26th and 27th October, 1979

Price 5p

*West Huntspill Players' programme for* Look Out For The Catch, *April 1978.*

*West Huntspill Players' programme for* Farewell, Farewell, Eugene, *October 1979.*

*West Huntspill Players,* Farewell, Farewell, Eugene *by John Vari, October 1979.*
Left to right: *Jill Strachan, Dorothy Mitchell (seated), June Kirby, Gavin Morris, Janet Begbie, Tony Burridge, Mavourneen Orchard, Bert Jenkins, Esme Wills (seated).*

# PARISH COUNCIL

Parish Councils have existed in their present form for over a century, but now there are changes afoot which will enable them to take a more pro-active part in making things happen. Of course, this has to be an acceptable idea to the public and the role of Clerk would be more onerous than at present, if that is possible! The co-operation of Parish Councils, within a local area, to take on these added responsibilities, is one of the changes mooted. Parish Councils have traditionally worked in partnership with other parishes through the National and County Association of Local Councils as well as with the County Council and, originally, the Rural District Council and (since 1974) District Councils such as Sedgemoor.

The Parish Council's traditional orbit has been footpaths, bus shelters, seating, etc. Other notable works have been the re-establishment of the village pond on the Common, the purchase of land and building of the Ilex Play Area and the Parish Map site on the Common. At times of heightened concern, such as when plans for sewerage works, waste tips, etc. have been on the agenda, the Council has asked the public to express a view by the way of public meetings. Of course, not every call for a meeting has had negative implications; people have gathered together to discuss such events as the coronation and silver jubilee.

Parish Councillors do not get paid. The hours devoted to Council business come from a genuine community spirit. There has never been any hint of party politics. The office of Chairman has, remarkably, been held by just a few people over the last 30 years of the 20th century; Mr F.C. Edwards, Mr W.C. Parkhouse (for more than one term) and Mrs J.A.K. Tiley (for an astounding 25 years without a break). The Chairman's role is made far easier by the presence of a good Clerk. There have been few changes to this post over the period and the Parish Council has benefited from their skills and dedication. Mr A. Lee (who had previously been a Parish Councillor), Mrs A. Smith and Mrs K. Gascoigne have all served as Clerks, between them covering the above-mentioned 30-year period. They were followed in quick succession by Mrs M. Butcher, Mrs E. Shaw (now Clerk to Burnham and Highbridge Town Council), Mrs L. Dicker and presently Mr T. Graham. The future looks to be more regulated but also a time in which opportunities will be created for the establishment of more services and facilities for the parish community.

# WEST HUNTSPILL WELCOME CLUB

The Welcome Club was formed (in conjunction with WRVS) on 14 January 1971. Miss Dors was elected Club Leader, with Mrs Audrey Vickery as Secretary and Mrs Rita Bird as Treasurer. The object of the club was to provide a social afternoon twice a month for the Over-Sixties of the village. This was very well supported by West Huntspill people for many years, and is still popular to this day, with membership extending as far as Highbridge and Burnham-on-Sea.

Originally a choir was formed, which provided much entertainment for members, and together with outings and annual holidays all made for a prosperous and enjoyable club. In 1977 a magnolia tree was planted in the churchyard by Mrs E. Palmer to commemorate the Queen's Silver Jubilee celebrations. The rector, Revd A. Virgin, officiated at the ceremony. Members enjoyed several holidays at Llandudno, joining with other local WRVS clubs to hire a coach for the week. They also ran day outings during the summer months, one per year being free to members, which took them as far afield as Prinknash Abbey, Southampton, the Welsh Mountains and Bourton on the Water.

*Jenefer Tiley, Chairman of West Huntspill Parish Council, presents a set of knockdown stumps to the Cricket Club on behalf of the Parish Council, July 2000.*

During the year an Easter Bonnet Competition was held, as also was a Craft and Flower Show, the member with most points holding the cup for the year. A Harvest Service was also held when members of other WRVS clubs were invited to join West Huntspill for the afternoon. In later years (until its closure) patients from Blake Hospital, Bridgwater, with their wheelchair attendants, joined the club for its service, when all were presented with gifts of fruit. At the time of writing the club officers are Club Leader Mrs Irene Austwick, Secretary Miss Anne Heayes (daughter of a former licensee of the Globe Inn, now the Scarlet Pimpernel), and Treasurer Mrs Ruby Major (daughter-in-law of two founder members). Members still follow the original format with a variety of speakers, vocalists, country and western entertainers, etc., together with talks and demonstrations on varied subjects. Members are also entertained by talent within the club. They run a raffle and auction at every meeting to augment their finances and every member receives a card on their birthday, special celebrations being marked with a party and a gift. In the year 2000 the club celebrated two diamond weddings, the happy couples being presented with gifts of champagne.

Members' family names include: Aish, Allen, Bird, Bishop, Clist, Day, Derham, Doble, Dors, Fry, Greener, Haggett, Jones, Lee, Major, Martin, Neath, Needs, Palmer, Parkhouse, Randle, Vickery, Viner, Vowles and Wade.

*The Welcome Club's decorated-hat competition at a club meeting in the Balliol Hall.*

*The Welcome Club's Easter bonnets (unisex), outside the Balliol Hall.*

*Welcome Club group holiday to Llandudno.*

# WOMEN'S INSTITUTE

Although the original record of the inaugural meeting of the West Huntspill WI held in 1951 has been lost, the following ladies were among the founder and early members: Ivy Cavill, Marjorie Cavill, Kath Haggett, Mary Hopkins, Edith Palmer, Gwen Porter, Freda Richardson and Nora Vinnecombe. Muriel Dors was both a founder member and also the first President. At the time of writing, two of these ladies are still members today, a quite remarkable feat as the WI celebrates its 50th anniversary this year – 2001. During the last 50 years the Institute has had many laughs, learnt a lot, enjoyed successes, made pounds of jam and sung 'Jerusalem' hundreds of times!

In 1970 a small committee was formed under the chairmanship of Edith Palmer to run a Spring Show. The event would be an open show with entries from the surrounding area. Muriel Dors was the show's first Secretary and entries for classes in flower arranging, plants, homecraft, handicraft, photography and children's work were organised. The show has gone from strength to strength and is now one of the highlights of the WI calendar. The West Huntspill Playgroup also provides a colourful display of work. With the frenetic organisation that it entails, before every Spring Show members find themselves asking 'is it worth it?' At the end of every hugely successful event with a record number of entries and a very high standard maintained they invariably come to the conclusion 'of course it is' and immediately start planning the next year's show!

As part of the WI's community involvement, members have provided a ripple bed for Burnham Memorial Hospital. To commemorate their 21st anniversary in 1972 they donated a clock to the Balliol Hall and it is still ticking 29 years later! They planted a silver birch tree at the Memorial Playing Fields for their 25th anniversary in 1976 but sadly that has not survived the years. In 1977 on the occasion of the Queen's Silver Jubilee, they put on picnic teas for all the children at the village celebrations. In 2001 members donated a wrought-iron seat to the village which will also be in memory of one of their most loyal members, Jenefer Tiley.

May 1989 saw the WI providing overnight accommodation for a mother and son who were travelling by pony and trap from John o' Groats to Land's End to raise funds for leukaemia. A member's daughter entered into the spirit of the occasion and cleaned the pony's tack until it gleamed. Members take an active part in a variety of village activities and help with the local school, Parish Council, Playgroup, children's clinic, charity work and the local churches – to name but a few. They have also been well represented on group and county committees.

Their sporting activities include skittle matches, ten-pin bowling, golf croquet, rambles and short-mat bowls, whilst several members have attended the National Federation of WI's own educational facility, Denman College, on a variety of courses. West Huntspill WI always looks forward to entertaining other local WIs at their annual party and enjoy hosting WI group carol services and group meetings. The entertaining items included in these group meetings always provide a lot of laughs. This was especially true on the occasion when four appropriately dressed ladies stood in an old tin bath which was filled with a murky mauve mixture and solemnly recited verses about 'Treading the Grapes'. Another member threw in buckets of 'grapes' whilst the four continued treading them in their bare feet! The WI has many gifted craftswomen whose skills range from ceramics, découpage, embroidery, pergomano, sugar craft, as well as knitting and needlework. Many members have exhibited at local, group and county level. West Huntspill is especially proud of three members, Margaret Budden, Ann Smith and Daphne Wilson, whose work was chosen to represent Somerset at a National Exhibition in 2000. At the time of writing the group is looking forward to their 50th celebrations. Sadly some events have had to be cancelled owing to outbreaks of foot and mouth disease, but other events are planned and members will no doubt continue to enjoy the friendship of the WI for many more years to come.

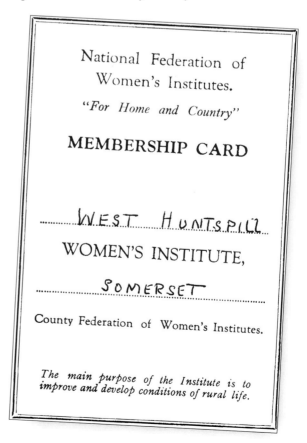

*WI membership card for 1951, the inaugural year.*

## Women's Institute

*West Huntspill WI 1st anniversary celebrations, November 1952. West Huntspill WI plus friends from Pawlett WI with the West Huntspill Girls Friendly Society are in the front row. Miss Muriel Dors is seated in the centre of the third row. The Revd Kevin Harrison and Mr Reg Clark are standing at the back.*

*West Huntspill WI 1st anniversary, November 1952. Miss Dors, Founder Member and President, is cutting the cake. Some of the other ladies in the photo including founder members are: Gwen Porter, Amy Dors, Vi Holley, Edith Palmer, Marjorie Cavill, Mrs Shepherd, Mrs Kate Allen, Miss Orpen.*

## Women's Institute

*West Huntspill WI 21st anniversary celebrations, 1972. The Committee and Miss Dors are cutting the cake. Committee members include: Edith Palmer, Edith Holmes, Vi Holley, Nora Vinnecombe, Mary Barton, Olwen MacCormack, Beryl Baker, Mary Gillard, Betty Lambert and ? Grayson.*

*West Huntspill WI 40th anniversary celebrations, November 1991. Nora Vinnecombe is seated on the left, and was presented with a gift prior to her emigration to Australia. Left to right, standing at the back: Freda Richardson and Mary Hopkins; seated centre: Gwen Porter; and standing in front: Kath Haggett. All of the ladies in the photo are either founder members or early members.*

*West Huntspill WI Spring Show, 1977. Jean Davis, Vi Holley and Kath Haggett are arranging the Homecraft exhibits.*

*West Huntspill WI members planting a silver birch in the churchyard, March 1995, in memory of founder member Gwen Porter. Left to right: Revd Geof. Walsh, Committee member Janet O'Neill, President Monica Hall, and early member Mary Hopkins.*

# ROYAL BRITISH LEGION

For many years there was a very strong branch of the Royal British Legion in the village. A Men's Section was formed in 1947 to be followed later by a Women's Section. The Branch unfortunately closed in the mid seventies when membership dwindled. Originally, the Branch met at the village school and held their annual suppers there. Later the meeting-place changed to the playing fields pavilion. The Branch met monthly. Each year a Garden Fête was held at the home of Mr Reg Clarke at Greenwood Farm. On two separate occasions outings to the Poppy Factory at Maidenhead were organised. Group meetings and other social occasions were attended by the Branch and these were at the homes of Senior Officers in the county.

The Women's Section organised the Annual Poppy Appeal

from 1948, at first under the eye of Mrs Wade. In 1966 Mrs Kath Haggett took over until the Branch closed. Mr Frank Davis and Mr Dennis Harrison then continued with the Appeal arrangements until 1983 when Mrs Monica Hall took over as the Poppy Appeal Organiser. In 1948 the price for the car mascot poppies was 2s.6d., whereas today the suggested donation is over £2. The village wreath in 1948 was priced at £1.6s., and today the cost of manufacture is £14.25. However, the good work of the Royal British Legion supporting members of the Forces and their families continues to this day. Conflicts around the world did not, unfortunately, end in 1945.

Left: *Royal British Legion, 1978. Mrs Kath Haggett presents a gold badge to Mrs J. Greener for services to the Royal British Legion, watched by Mrs Wade (sitting).*

*Royal British Legion annual dinner held at West Huntspill School, 30 November 1957. People present include: Ron and Mary Hopkins, Mr Hobbs, George and Annie Haggett, Francis Haggett, Mr Burrows, George Derham, Mr and Mrs J. Coombes, Mr and Mrs Roy Last, Mr Aubrey Lee, Dr McArthur, Mrs Greener, Jack Hobbs, Mrs Wade, Mr Edwards, Mr and Mrs Spellor, Len Inder.*

*Youth Club outing to Ilfracombe, 1947.*  Included in the photograph are: *Eddie Ham,*
*Elma Riggs, Mary Sandy, Olive Sandy, Ron Hopkins and Mrs Joyce Derham holding her baby son.*

# YOUTH CLUB

A Youth Club, held in the Balliol Hall, was started by
Vincent Derham in 1946 when he returned from the
Navy after serving in the Second World War.  The
membership was approximately 70 with members
from East and West Huntspill and Highbridge.
Activities consisted of snooker, table tennis,
boxing, fencing and billiards.  Subscription was 6d.
per session, whilst the rent for the hall was 4
shillings.  Members, who were required to be 14
years of age or over, were expected to support club
activities and generally help take part in running the
group.  Members of the club were also expected to
attend the St George's Day Service in the local church
(although in fact many were members of the
congregation anyway).

Each year trips to other clubs and outings
to seaside resorts were arranged, as also was an
annual visit to London, where members stayed at
the Youth Hostel in Bedford Square.  The trip cost
£2.10s. and members saved a shilling each week
for the trip which was paid into the club funds.  The
trip consisted of two nights in the Youth Hostel
with breakfast and the ticket for a first-class show
in the West End.  The coach fare was also included
in the price.  The club was very successful.  On
coronation day in 1953 members organised and paid
for the evening celebrations for the village.

In 1954, after the Derham family moved away,
interest in the club dwindled and it finally closed.
During the 1980s Christine and Tony Baker, together
with the help of others, formed another Youth Club
in the Balliol Hall which ran successfully for five
years.  Membership figures were in the region of 50
to 60 children.  The club took part in many activities
and competitions including table tennis, darts and
uni-hock (indoor hockey with a soft puck).  Finally
the Youth Club closed, once again because of lack of
support.  An attempt was made to re-form it two
years later but this was not successful.

# MINIATURE STEAM RAILWAY

The Miniature Steam Railway was opened at the
Playing Field in 1967 and has been carrying passengers on Sunday afternoons in the Playing Field for
more than 25 years.  Mr Len Foster, a member of the
Weston-Super-Mare and West Huntspill Live Steam
Society (Miniature Railway), also gave much
pleasure to the local Playgroup members when he
kindly ran the locomotives especially for the children
during a Playgroup outing to the Playing Fields.  The
original members met in Weston–Super-Mare at the
home of Mort Street, who made them very welcome
in the 'railway shed' in his garden.  The devoted
enthusiasts put thousands of hours into making the

**SOMERSET & DORSET MEMORIAL**
# Miniature Railway

# OPENING DAY
## SATURDAY, 12th AUGUST, 1967

**THE PLAYING FIELDS, NEW ROAD
WEST HUNTSPILL, Nr. HIGHBRIDGE**

**THE NEW TRACK WILL BE OPENED BY
H. L. SHEPARD, Esq.    -    at 3.0 p.m.**

Steam Trains will then be run over the track which is $3\frac{1}{2}''$ and $5''$ gauge and one-tenth of a mile long

## Weston-super-Mare and West Huntspill
## LIVE STEAM SOCIETY

PATEY & CO., PRINTERS, BURNHAM-ON-SEA.

*Miniature Railway Opening Day poster, 12 August 1967.*

*Opening of the Miniature Railway at the New Road Playing Field by Mrs Sheperd, 1967.*

engines. The society was formed in the early 1960s and just grew! Thanks to Len Foster, when the club outgrew the garden 'railway shed', wheels were put in motion to approach West Huntspill Parish Council with a view to using an area of the Playing Fields. The Chairman of the Parish Council at that time was Mr Sheperd who was very enthusiastic and a great help.

The building of the railway at West Huntspill dates from about 1966 and was opened in 1967. The sleepers, which came from the Somerset & Dorset yard at Highbridge, and the track were laid on a raised concrete bed. This was when local people, including the Hawkins family, Ted Lambert and others, got involved with the project. The track can accommodate three-and-a-half- to five-inch-gauge engines that are capable of hauling trains of passengers who sit on flat bed trucks that straddle the track. The locomotives which are all hand built by the members are fired by Welsh steam coal. They are in every way faithful reproductions of their larger brothers, responding in exactly the same way. The station building which was brought from Evercreech had been a station shelter on the Somerset & Dorset line. The present members work hard to maintain the track in good order and it is good to see the enthusiasm still there, both with them and the public

passengers – of all ages. An article in the *Weston Mercury* of February 1981 which was reporting on the Society's Annual Exhibition held at the Orchard Inn, quoted Mr Mort Street as saying:

*I think steam locomotives have a fascination about them that no other transport has, I mean what's an electric engine? Nothing more than a glorified tram. And a diesel locomotive is just an engine in a box, but steam, well, it's so simple you just have to boil water to provide the power.*

Mr Mort Street added: 'If you've got steam in your blood then you've got it forever.'

## OTHER PAST CLUBS

An Old Time and Sequence Dance Club was formed in 1971 and met in the Balliol Hall. It survived at least until the late 1970s. There was a Branch of The Loyal Order of Moose, Lodge No.208, which met at the Balliol Hall until the mid 1980s. A Tennis Club was formed in the 1950s and later disbanded and although an attempt was made in the mid 1970s to re-start it this failed.

## Chapter Nine

# FAMILY HISTORIES & REMINISCENCES

The following is quoted from the *Huntspill News* of June 2001;

## TONY BAKER – POLICEMAN AND CHURCHWARDEN

*Tony never planned to be a policeman. Born in Barking in Essex, the son of a Navy family, he spent most of his young life globe-trotting. He lived in Malta and Australia and went to school near Sydney. He completed his education in England and was accepted to read pure maths, applied maths and physics at Cardiff University. However, Tony, in his own words, 'spent too much time partying,' and had to leave! He had already met Chris, his future wife, and while she finished her university career he began the long hard search for a job. In one of the worst recessions for years, and after sixty-four applications, he started work in a high-class jewellers. His next career move was to one of the first DIY superstores, but he was starting to tire of selling bathrooms when Chris introduced him to her uncle who was a policeman.*

### From Hippy to Sergeant

*Tony laughed when it was suggested that he might join the police force. He describes himself as an 'ex hippy', hardly suitable material for the police, but he went for an interview in Taunton. He was accepted, and twenty-eight years later admits it was the job for him! He and Chris moved a great deal – Bath, Frome, Mells – he loved Mells: 'his own little patch with his own little station', but promotion beckoned and he moved on to Wells, then Glastonbury. Here one of his jobs was as 'Schools Liaison Officer' based at Crispin School, Street. The work was hard but varied. He remembers giving a talk at Millfield School in a large lecture theatre containing 300 students!*

### Challenged by Christianity

*Policing is not an easy job and Tony was often confronted by suffering humanity: people in pain, injured and shocked, asking, 'WHY ME?' He noticed that some people coped better than others and began to realise that this was due to their faith. By now he had*

*been promoted to sergeant, was working in Weston-super-Mare and was looking for somewhere to live. He and Chris came to Huntspill, fell in love with the village, and moved to their present home. Encouraged by Chris, he became involved with the church. His curiosity changed to belief and he started working with the Sunday School and other youth groups. Although afraid of heights, to raise funds he has abseiled (partly upside down) down the church tower, an experience he describes as more terrifying than facing a rioting mob with petrol bombs in Bristol. Being a practising Christian and a policeman is not easy, but when Tony was appointed Churchwarden he felt he was able to 'give something back to the church on a practical level.' He has served the church faithfully for six years in this capacity and, two years from his retirement from the police force, we in the parish thank him for all he has done for us.*

## THE DERHAM FAMILY, WEST HUNTSPILL, 1916–PRESENT

*by Peter Derham*

My grandfather Henry Charles Derham (1871–1933) was born at Haymoor End, Knappe, North Curry in Somerset. He moved to South Wales as a young man to work in the coal mines, rising to manager at Six Bells Colliery, Aberbeeg. Upon retiring, with silicosis, in 1916 he became landlord of the Globe Hotel, West Huntspill. Henry came to Huntspill with his wife Annie Selena (née Thomas) and his six children: George, Reginald, William, May, Eunice and Bessie. After his death in 1933 his wife Annie ran the Globe until her death in 1944, after which time the pub was run by the youngest son, William, until 1949. William was quite a character and at that time his motto was 'We are never closed', which reminds me of a tale with regard to one keen cider-drinking customer between the wars who arrived in his horse and trap, drank until he fell over and was then put back in his trap. Dolly the horse was given a pat and would then find his own way home.

*Henry Charles Derham and family, c.1918.*

George Derham married Amy. They had three children: Freda (Richardson), Vincent and Michael. George fought in the First World War and followed the family to West Huntspill with Amy and their children in 1926. He spent his working life as a salesman dealing in consumer goods and was reputed to have known every blade of grass in the area. George was also well known for playing the piano at local social functions and as an accompanist to the silent movies. All three children attended the local school.

Freda married Roy Richardson and they had two children, Steve and Janet. Freda is well known in the village and over the years has done much good work with many of the village activities. They live near the village main road.

Vincent Derham is married to Ronnie. They have three children: Jane, Mary and Mark. He has five children from a previous marriage, four of which were born in the village. Vincent served in the Navy during the Second World War and is well known as a local Councillor and ex Mayor of Burnham and Highbridge. He gives much support to village activities. Vincent and Ronnie live in a cottage in the village, next door to their daughter Jane, husband Roy and their children. Mary is married to Paul and lives in Weston. Mark is married to Vivien and lives in Brent Knoll.

Michael Derham has four children and lives in the next village of Mark.

Essie Derham married Cyril Sedgbeer and they had two children and lived in Alstone Lane.

Eunice Derham lived and worked at the Globe Hotel during the tenure of the Derham family and married Samuel Tuck in later life. As a widow at age 61 she learnt to drive and then drove for 30 years. She lived for some years in Smurl Lane.

Reginald Derham (my father) married Joan Baby and lived for some years in Alstone Lane, next door to sister Essie. He had four children: Diana, Peter, David and Julian. Reg attended the local school from his arrival in the village in 1916 aged nine years until his 14th birthday. He was a bell-ringer in his youth, in between roaring around the countryside on his 500cc motorcycle. Reg served two stints in the Army before and during the Second World War after which he was well known as a bus driver on local routes.

Diana Derham married Derek Batt and has four children. Although she lives in Burnham, she is known in the village as a member of the local drama group.

Peter Derham married Barbara Smith from Burnham and has two sons: Christopher and Paul. Peter was born in the village. The telegram sent from West Huntspill Post Office announcing his birth, to his father Reg serving in the Army in France in December 1939, from his grandmother Annie still exists. Peter attended the local school and spent his working life building helicopters and is now retired.

## The Derham Family

The Globe Hotel with Mr Derham
and son Reg, 1920s.

Telegram dating from 1939
announcing the birth of
Peter Derham.

Reg Derham on his 500cc
BSA motorbike, c.1936.

Reg Derham on his 80th birthday,
13 August 1986. He is sitting in
a period bus hired for the occasion.
A party was held at the Scarlet
Pimpernel which was renamed the
Globe Hotel for the day.

Peter and Barbara have lived their married life in the same house in Church Road for the last 35 years, where their sons were born. Christopher and Paul Derham attended the local school and grew up in the village, playing football and cricket for the local teams. Christopher is married to Noreen and with baby son Sean lives in Weybridge. Paul lives in Boston, USA, with partner Tiggy.

David and Julian Derham were both born in the village. David spent his working life in the aircraft industry and is now retired living in Weston. Julian has two children. He had a career in the RAF and now lives and works in Weston. The following family members are resting in the local churchyard: Henry and Annie Derham, George and Amy Derham, Reg Derham, Essie and daughter Doreen, Eunice Tuck, Steve Richardson (son of Freda and Roy).

## HOOPERS' MILK ROUND

Since 24 October 1924 there has been a milk round in the village run by the Hooper family. Originally the family lived in Alstone Lane but in 1930 Granny Hooper rented Laburnum House in Sloway Lane for her two daughters, Mrs Gladys Boon and Miss Beatrice Hooper. The two ladies continued to run the round together from Sloway Lane for many years until the death of Gladys in 1966. Miss Hooper, who had by then been joined on the round by Mrs Boon's son John, continued with the round until her death in 1991. John had joined the family business after leaving school and still runs the round today.

Until the mid seventies, the only day the family had off was Christmas Day, deliveries on Sundays continuing until then. Floods, snow and road closures have not prevented the family from making daily deliveries. Milk deliveries continued from Sloway Lane until 1981 when the flood of that year forced a move. A change of location had been in the pipeline but when the property was flooded out a move was inevitable. Today, 77 years after the start of the round, deliveries are organised from a property in Huntspill Road, Highbridge. Many villagers have been having their milk delivered by the family firm for over 60 years. The fact that the Hoopers' and John Boon's milk round is a village institution is illustrated by this tale from Playgroup. The children were asked, 'where does milk come from?' The reply, after a pause, 'Johnny Boon'; — 'yes, but where does John Boon get his milk from?' The reply to this: 'his van'!

*Laburnum House, 1970s. John Boon and his aunt, Miss Hooper, ran their*
*milk-delivery business from their home here until the flood in the early 1980s.*

# THE SAUNDERS FAMILY

*by Jean Saunders*

I was born in 1937, the fifth child in the family, in a small cottage, Myrtle Cottage in Catherine Street. I was a few weeks old when Mum fell victim to the typhoid epidemic that hit West Huntspill village; many people died, but luckily my Mum survived after spending six months in the Isolation Hospital at Axbridge. When Mum left the hospital we were given a new house in Ringstone where year after year Mum gave birth to another eight children. In all she had seven boys and six girls – what an enormous task!

I was very young during the war years but I can remember the blackouts (covering windows if you had a light on) and the ration books for butter, cheese, bacon and clothing, etc. There were many wartime evacuees sent to our village and my grandmother, who lived nearby, had a little girl who we grew to love as our own. She had been evacuated to West Huntspill from Russell Square in London. Living in a big family was really quite lovely and lots of other local children loved to come and play with us – my Mum was a very kind lady. Going out to play, as I got older, we used our imagination to create our own adventures; playing in Stoney Path, making pretend houses or making our own May Festival in the field near our house and at the same time looking after my younger brothers and sisters. A lot of our activities centred around the Methodist Chapel and a dedicated Superintendent, Mr Frank Cavill, was a kind man to us children. Lots of the evacuees came to Sunday School where we had lots of competitions with real prizes and one evening a week Bible class. Miss Heal (now Mrs Wesley Cavill) took the class, a bunch of lively children wanting to talk about everything except the Bible – she had such tolerance. Once a year we had the chapel outing to Clevedon; with great excitement we waited for the charabanc. On the anniversary of the chapel we had our chapel prizes, always a nice book, only one of mine has survived with me. At harvest time we filled our chapel with fruit and veg and always had a special large loaf displayed, which Mr Cavill always gave to my Mum. At Christmas time groups of us would go singing carols around the village. We would sing loudest for a few coppers. We also had a chapel party every year – a lovely tea and party games followed. The Girls Friendly Society was held at the Balliol Hall and I joined with lots of other friends. Two very extraordinary ladies ran it; they lived in Smurl Lane, two sisters, the Misses Taylor. We learned many creative skills from them and they also taught us to make our own bamboo pipes. Then eventually we played them in our own band.

In springtime we could walk down Withy Road and on into Puriton Road via Black Ditch and pick arms full of cowslips and cuckoo flowers; they graced Mum's table many, many times. In the summer we would, as a family, walk to Burnham beach for the day and in September we often went blackberrying, and could sell the fruit for a few coppers a lb to the man, Albie Hicks, who came around to collect them. Many's the time he would accuse us of adding water to increase the weight, hence more money. We would also walk to the sea wall to swim in the pools the sea left behind. Sometimes it seemed quite stagnant – but it didn't seem to hurt us. Lovely, lovely days.

I started school when I was very young, three-and-a-half years old, in the schoolroom of the Balliol Hall. Shirley Wilson, my grandmother's evacuee, took me there. I can just remember the little rounded rung-backed chairs. I dare say I was there because of Mum's large family. There were some advantages being one of a large family. At the age of five I attended West Huntspill school with Miss Ferguson being my first teacher. I remember the bright and happy classroom we had. Miss Phillips, my next teacher, was so lovely – she used to have me to tea with her. She lived in part of Mr Arney's house on the corner of Alstone Lane. I loved school and was very eager to learn but the trouble was my position in the family, and being a girl meant I was very helpful to my Mum as I was used to looking after my younger brothers and sisters. I had to have a day off school on Mum's big wash days to give her a hand; I used to feel disappointed but not for long. I loved my brothers and sisters.

The teacher who had most impact on me at school was a man named Mr Cyril Parish, from Pawlett. He was a teacher that really respected children and he recognised my Mum's struggle to bring up a large family and sometimes pointed out to the whole class that you didn't need material things in life to shine. The Headmaster, Mr Davey, was a disciplinarian who was greatly feared for the use of his cane. Some people have said he was well respected, but I think that's a misconception; he ruled with a rod of iron and we were scared of him.

In winter time we had only one coke stove to heat the big classroom and often we had to keep our coats on in class to keep warm. Mind you, it used to thaw our free milk out, which we were given daily.

We had a very successful netball team, for which I played centre, competing against all other schools in the district. One day a week we had to travel by bus to the Burnham Tec. for cookery lessons with Miss Lovecote. If she had any problems with our class, she would ride her motorbike down to Huntspill School to lodge her complaint to Mr Davey in person. If we knew somebody had to go before the Headmaster for something or other, we shivered in our shoes. After a busy day at school it was good to run home and be greeted with a thick slice of Mum's steamed pudding smothered in jam. Happy days.

## *The Saunders Family*

*The Saunders family, 1988.
Left to right, back: Pat, Terry;
middle: Sue, Christine,
David, John, Mark, Richard;
front: Irene, Keith,
Valerie, Jean, Graham.*

*The Princess Royal speaks
to Army Cadet Lee
Saunders on her visit
to Burnham-on-Sea,
July 1988.*

# Growing Up in West Huntspill

*by Graham Saunders*

I was born in February 1942 into a large family of 13; six brothers and six sisters. Some of my earliest memories of village life was the fish man Mr Powell and his daughter coming to the village with all kinds of fresh fish, sometimes giving the odd cat or two a fish head, then the peat turf lorry would arrive selling turf for the fire, then the coal lorry, the milk lady on her bike with a trailer on the back and taking a measuring jug to the door to fill our own jugs. I remember going with my older brothers to Highbridge (walking) to fetch coal briquettes and also going to Mr Inders the local undertakers with our bucket for lime to paint out the larder.

The year 1947 was a very hard winter; it even froze the river over and some of the local kids made their own sledges and went down one bank across the ice to the other side which was good fun – dangerous, but still good fun. The snow was very deep but did not last long. The local school was closed for a short while. In the summer it was mud slides down the banks in the same place.

We would have to take the accumulators over to Mr Baker to be charged for the wireless, and then fetch paraffin for the oil lamps. I can just remember Mr Hobbs at the Crossways Inn, Mr Derham at the Globe Inn, Mr Jones at the Post Office, Mr Napten the postman, Mr Fowler at the shop, Mr Cavell at Ilex Nursery, Colonel Handcock at Swell House, Mr Baker the blacksmith, Mr Palmer in the Mill, Mr Harvey and Chas Day the local builders, Mr Eveley the bike repairer, Mr Williams' first shop at the Crossways then later in the cottage opposite what is now Forge Close, Mr and Mrs Greener at Huntspill Court, Mr and Mrs Peddy at the old forge on the Common, Mr Clark JP at Greenwood Lodge, Mr Davey the schoolmaster and the rector Vere Hodge.

Looking back some of the things we got up to were quite dangerous, like the time we would go on the railway lines to put halfpennies on the track to flatten them to try to make them look like pennies; the driver of the train would sometimes report us when he arrived at Highbridge, then it would not be long before the police were after us. Then there would be another time when we would crawl through the culvert to get to the Mill (culvert on main road). As kids we often made our own things like whistles from withy, also bows and arrows from reeds with elder tips (again very dangerous), and catapults made from ash branches. I also remember the blacksmith making large hoops and attaching a handle to the hoop so as the large hoop would pass through the handle, it was possible to make the hoop move forward keeping it upright. We would run to the shops for the older people – first for the money then for the coupons to get two ounces of sweets.

At school, infants class was taught by Mrs Ferguson, a lovely lady. I remember the band instruments very well – the drums, cymbals and triangle. I was always over enthusiastic when playing the drums and so then I was hastily moved and ended up playing the triangle. In the afternoons we would have to have a rest and this would be on coconut matting and with no pillows! Often we would run out the doors straight into the bomb blast walls which were just in front of the main doors, which at a later date were removed.

As you progressed up through the classes you became responsible for collecting your replacement pencils, rubbers, books and nibs for the pens, and you would have to line up outside the headmaster's room one morning a week. There could be as many 20 children outside his room at one time and you had better not be wasting his time. For example, if you could still write with the pencil it did not need replacing; a rubber would have to be the size of a pea (but just imagine dropping a rubber the size of a pea onto a hard floor). Pandemonium would break loose to try and find it quickly before it was your turn to go into his room. Some of the headmaster's comments regarding what you were bringing in would sound like this, for a rubber – 'you've made a lot of mistakes haven't you', for a nib – 'try writing with it instead of trying to stick it in the top of your desk', for a pencil – 'you like using the pencil sharpener do you!', with a book he would remark about the 'dog ears' on the corners of the old book.

The school dentist would call and this would be at Miss King's house in New Road, then the nit nurse would arrive. We all had good fun when they were building the new dining room and the extra classroom. The pitch they used for the floors would be made into marbles and everybody had pitch marbles, some small, some large – you can imagine the fun we all had with those. Playing post in the playground was fun for some but not all, you would have two teams by jumping onto bent-over backs and you would take it in turns to see if you could make the other team collapse before the last one jumped on and before the bell would ring for lunch.

Before the dining hall was built you would have to go and get your dinner from the headmaster's room and go and eat it at your desk (the dinners were brought in already cooked from a Council-run kitchen).

At home we did not have electric light; when we were young it was paraffin lamps and Mother would shout 'close the door steady' as it would break the glass globe on the lamp. Cooking was done on a range with an open fire and one oven, also with primus stoves, and all washing was done by hand, the hot water for the washing being done by lighting up the furnace and then bailing the water out of the furnace into a tin bath. Mum was well known for her very white sheets, I think it was the blue bags in the final rinse that did the trick. I can see her now wringing out the sheets twisting up her arm and then out to the mangle. After the washing there was the floors to polish with red cardinal polish, and did they shine! No carpets in our house, you had to have a head for heights to just clean the windows. Mum would sit on the windowsill to clean the outside top windows. The gypsies would camp on the Common and make their clothes pegs out of withy sticks which they had helped themselves to around the area. Mr Webb would park his steam-roller at the end of the elms on the Common, and that was a good place to play! I can also remember on a couple of occasions the water pumps working in the drought.

# A HUNTSPILL CHILDHOOD

## *by Mark Saunders*

By the time I came along my parents were quite used to having children around the house, as I am the youngest of 13, and being so, I was born into this world being the 13th child of the 13th child, also the 7th son of the 7th son, which to some people seems to be quite relevant and important. I remember very early in life that it was most important that the workers at the house had to be fed first in the mornings. It is very difficult to imagine 13 children sat around a table but it used to happen. Obviously, the milk jug held ½ gallon, the salt was a whole block (cut lump), which had to be scraped with a knife, and the tea pot took Mother two hands to hold whilst pouring. Everything in our house had to be on catering scale, even so, Mum kept the house spotless, we even helped with the polishing. Mum would tie dusters on our feet and let us slide around the living room as though roller skating; boy did that lino shine.

Because we were a very large family we only had the necessities to survive. Luxuries were definitely out but we did have a few home-made treats. Mum used to make lactic cheese from sour milk which she used to hang on the washing line in a stocking so it would drain and set. Ice-cream was made when it used to snow. We would fill a cup with fresh snow, add 'evap. milk', a little sugar and hey presto beautiful ice-cream. I never felt envious of other kids as everyone was in the same situation; as a matter of fact I think we were better off in certain ways.

Life was never boring; there was always something to do, or places to go. A lot of things we did were centred around the seasons and time of year. Birds nesting in the spring meant duck and moorhen eggs, which of course were taken home where they were cooked and eaten, and we had jars for frogspawn. Summertime was for fishing, building dens and playing hide and seek in the long grass. Autumn was the season of plenty – apples, soft fruit (not our own of course, we just knew where to get it) and wild mushrooms. The highlight of the autumn was always the Flower Show which used to last almost a week; that's if you take into account the days we would wait in the copse opposite the Post Office waiting for 'Tacker' Ron

Burroughs who would arrive always on the Thursday with his old grey lorry loaded with the marquee. Within ten minutes of him arriving, the field would be swarming with kids helping to lay out the ropes, poles and canvas. When the marquee was eventually pulled up it was massive; it seemed a mile high by a mile long. In those days the Flower Show was a mini fair, it was wonderful. Winter was when we would take the ferret and get off for a few rabbits; we would eat a few and sell a few, that is until Dad sold the ferret.

My next eldest brother, my nephews Steve and Rob and I, were the original gang of four, and we were all about the same age. For a year or two we would spend all day away from home having different adventures every day. If mums and dads knew what we were up to they would have a fit – like on spring tides actually wading across the Parrett at low tide to Steart Island to collect a few seagull eggs, or as many as we could carry, anyway. Or playing hide and seek in farmer House's kale crop. Or pinching Bill Greener's prize plums, but we never took more than we could carry. Those days really did seem long and the sun did always shine. If I could have my childhood again I wouldn't change anything, such wonderful times.

My earliest recollection of school days was being in the infants class. My teacher was Mrs Clarke, an elderly lady who lived in Poorhouse Lane (Church Road) just past the present Orchard Inn. She rode a bicycle to school which was a huge thing with a wicker basket on the front. I can vaguely remember having the honour of fetching it before school was out and having to wheel it around the front ready for her to ride home. One thing she used to do was collect all the sweets that she was given. She kept them in an oval-shaped date box. Then when we had a reading or writing test, she would give out those sweets, as prizes, only one each. I never had a toffee or blackjack chew, it was always an aniseed ball which I was always told off for sucking too hard. Another task which I was given was scraping up the flattened blobs of plasticine from the wooden floor with a blunt knife. I used to end up with a filthy ball of plasticine about the size of a tennis ball which was promptly thrown in the bin. One of my pet hates was when she made me blow my nose in newspaper when I had the sniffs. At this time, in the mid 1950s, you started school at five years and left when you were fourteen or fifteen. So to me it seemed as though the people in the top class were adults. But, as I was the youngest from a family of six brothers and six sisters, it seemed to me as though I had a member of the family in each class and at this time was watched over by them to make sure I came to no harm (being the baby of the family).

At dinner time the small ones were always in at second sitting in the dining room. Mrs Derront the dinner lady always gave me two dollops of spud. The only thing about school dinners I didn't like was the smell of the cooked cabbage but I always ate everything that was put on my plate. Dinner break seemed to last about three hours. PE was done in the empty dinner hall on coconut mats with all instruction coming from the old radio in the corner. The older members of the school used to dig the garden and plant vegetables. That was for the boys, I never knew what the girls did!

One of the best things that happened while I was at school was when they took away the wall which went across the playground at the back. Then we could play football without the big boys pinching our ball. Also we didn't have to walk all the way around the school to fill the coke bucket.

Other teachers I remember were Mrs Cox – she was a rather large lady. I think she was a nurse or St John's Ambulance, or something like that. I didn't like her very much as she seemed very strict. Mr Hoey – I don't know what subjects he taught, I can only remember him walking around the playground puffing on his pipe. Mr Derbyshire – he had a habit of rocking on his feet from one side to another. I think someone had mentioned to me that he was shot in the leg in the war. As kids we would believe anything. He was a very tall, upright, smart gentleman who used to say if he caught you talking, when you weren't supposed to, 'Boy I shall descend upon you from a dizzy altitude'. Huntspill School for me were good times; no complaints when I had the cane from the headmaster Mr Eastlake. On reflection I deserved it. At the age of 11 years it was off to Burnham new Secondary Modern; my childhood was over.

The following is quoted from the *Huntspill News* of May 2001:

## AT HOME WITH SYLVIA SIMS

*It was a great privilege to sit in Sylvia's sitting room, sipping Earl Grey tea, overlooking her sunny back garden. Somewhere, beneath a mass of roses and rosemary, trembled three traumatised hens, whose coop had been invaded the night before by a badger. In the corner of her garden stands a statue of St. Francis, a reminder of her interest in the Franciscan Way. She's been involved with the Franciscans since the nineties, when she went to a prayer workshop in Axbridge. There she met the inspirational wheelchair-bound Sister Angela Helen, dressed in her brown habit, fastened with a white cord.*

*Sister Angela told Sylvia about the three orders of the Franciscans. The First Order are those who live in their own community, but work outside it in order to finance themselves. The Second Order is a contemplative, closed one, which runs retreats. The Third Order founded by St. Francis himself, is also called the Order of Penitents, specifically for busy lay people who want to live the simple prayerful life of the Franciscans. Sylvia became a postulant, then a novice, finally professing in October 2000 as a member of the Third Order.*

*Sylvia has not always lived in Huntspill. She was born in Bath, where she attended a Grammar school. She was accepted to read music at St. Hugh's College, Oxford, and then having obtained her degree, studied for a Diploma in Education. Meanwhile she had met her husband David, an undergraduate at St. Johns, Oxford. They married and moved to Lancashire, where her eldest son Richard was born. Sylvia obtained a teaching post at Bolton School, but the family eventually moved onto Shirley in Warwickshire, where Jonnie and Lizzy were born. Another move to Letchworth saw the birth of Katy and Alex and her family was complete.*

### Jack Of All Trades

*Sylvia moved to Huntspill in 1988 to teach music. She describes herself as a 'jack of all trades.' She studied for a diploma in French, taught by her husband and has happy memories of these lessons, David smoking a cigar, mugs of beer at their elbows. Always seeking to broaden her knowledge, she gained a Science degree with the Open University. Recently she has taken up the cello and now coaches a quartet. To Sylvia, the Church has always been of special importance and despite her duties as choir mistress and assistant organist, she continued her self development by joining a Christian Foundation course. Here the seed of an idea was born and in her own words 'would not go away.' Having approached our Rector Geoffrey, he encouraged her to take up further training as a lay reader. With the backing of the Church and the PCC, she went for an interview and was accepted. On Palm Sunday Sylvia preached her first sermon.*

The following is quoted from the *Huntspill News* of July/August 2001:

## LES TURNER – A SON OF HUNTSPILL

*Les grew up in a Huntspill that few of us would recognise. His grandparents lived on the corner of Cadwells Lane, in a cottage with honeysuckle over the doors, while Les himself spent his early years in a cottage in Silver Street and then Withy Road. He attended Huntspill School, until he was fourteen, and remembers knocking the helmet off Constable Burfitt's head and being chased up to the sea wall and back by the irate policeman! He played the accordion and after leaving school became an apprentice plumber. In those days and in an area of dairy farming, much of his work was on farms, lining cattle drinking troughs and in the days of farm-produced cheese, installing and repairing dairy steam boilers.*

*At the beginning of the Second World War he enlisted in the Royal Engineers as a plumber and pipe fitter 3rd class, re-mustered after training in Belgium as 1st class and went on to become N.C.O. It was while he was stationed at Dover Castle that his life-long love affair with this place began. He has a fund of stories*

131

*about his war experiences. Storming the beaches in Normandy, he landed on D3. While marching inland he encountered an elderly French couple, strolling hand in hand. They exchanged the time of day as if nothing was happening! Les also saw action as a Sergeant in India, Malaya and Singapore.*

*With the war behind him, Les proposed to his beloved Ida and they were married in Weston, settling eventually in their lovely bungalow in Silver Street, in the vicinity of his childhood home. Here Ida created her beautiful garden and Les bred canaries. He still has a large aviary in his back garden, the birds like jewels in amber and gold. At this time of the year the wicker nesting boxes are full of tiny babies, which look just like Easter chicks!*

*They returned frequently to Dover, staying in their favourite hotel. But even in the best hotels, accidents can happen! Once the heating system broke down and no plumber was to be found. Ida volunteered her husband's services and clad in a borrowed boiler suit and with a few tools, Les sorted it out. That evening there was a complimentary bottle of wine on the table for them.*

*Les started his own small business, employing eight people, and was kept busy working in houses, schools, churches and small factories. He installed the heating system in the Balliol Hall and still maintains it. Last year, the Association of Plumbing, Heating and Mechanical Services Contractors, of which Les is past President and now secretary of the local branch, threw a surprise party for his 80th Birthday. In Les' own words 'the evening was marred for me without Ida standing beside me. Her passing was the greatest loss I have ever sustained.' Ida had tragically died in 1996 and her ashes are interred beside Les' parents in Huntspill churchyard.*

*Les says some day he will lie there too and when that time comes he would like to be remembered as 'Les Turner – Plumber to this Parish.'*

# THE PIZEY FAMILY

## by Vincent Derham

The Revd Pizey was the vicar of Mark and moved to West Huntspill in 1910 to become the rector of the village. The Revd Pizey and Mrs Pizey had two sons, Mark and Edward, and a daughter, Mary. The Pizey family were very much involved in village activities. The rector had a very good sense of humour. I can still remember being told as a child how he once entered the old School Room, which was then also the village hall, with a pair of ladies' bloomers on the end of his walking stick. He then asked the dancers who they belonged to as they had been found in the churchyard! When a young lady blushed, he said 'Ah, I know who they belong to, carry on and enjoy yourselves'!

Mrs Pizey used to collect the rent from the cottages which were then next to the hall. One day a bad smell came from one of the cottages and when the householder was asked what it was, the reply was given, 'Game is hung for a number of weeks so why shouldn't chicken be hung?'

Mary became a local schoolteacher whilst Mark and Edward joined the Royal Navy. Mark joined at the age of 12 and was later in the Battle of Jutland during the First World War. Mrs Pizey and Mary were very fond of the village children and would gather us on the Rectory lawn to give us strawberries and cream and other goodies. The Revd Pizey died on holiday in Scotland during 1932. The village lost a fine rector and the family moved out of West Huntspill. Various local families still maintained contact though with the Pizey family.

During the 1939 to 1945 war, Edward became Rear Admiral Portsmouth Division Submarines, whilst Mark, who was a senior officer in the Royal Navy, became the Commander in Chief Nore (East Coast and Thames Area) very early on in the war. Mark commanded the ships which tried to engage and prevent the two German Pocket battleships from passing through the English Channel. Later he became the Commander in Chief in Malta. After the war Mark was given charge of the Indian Navy when India became independent.

I can well remember a few months after the war ended, I brought a naval friend home on leave. We were walking along Church Road, West Huntspill, when a car drew up and Mrs Pizey spoke to me. She introduced her son Mark, who was in civilian clothes, to us. My friend and I were in naval uniforms and after a long conversation we went on our way. My friend remarked what nice people they were and who were they? When I explained that it was Mrs Pizey, the late Rector's wife and her son Rear Admiral Pizey, my friend was a little embarrassed thinking he had just told a Rear Admiral how to run the Navy!

Mark Pizey eventually became a full Admiral, was knighted and given many honours. In retirement he became a pig farmer and eventually retired, with Lady Pizey, to Burnham-on-Sea. Sir Admiral Mark Pizey died in 1993 at the age of 93. I was mayor of Burnham-on-Sea and Highbridge at the time and was honoured to attend the Remembrance Service on behalf of the Council. Lady Pizey predeceased Sir Mark some six weeks before his departure and both their ashes are interred with the Revd and Mrs Pizey in West Huntspill churchyard, adjacent to the church. I was privileged to know the Pizeys first as a small child, then as a young man and later in life when I was the Mayor. I was very proud to be recognised in my naval uniform as a young man by Mrs Pizey as she had not seen me for a number of years. The last time she had seen me I had still been a child. They were nice people.

*Chapter Ten*

# FARMS & PUBS

## FARMS

The basis of the community over the past millennium and beyond has been agriculture. There remain five working farms within the parish: Alstone Court Farm, Court Farm, Maundrils Farm, Plymor Hill Farm and Poplar Farm. There is a sixth, Brue Farm, which falls within the town boundary of Highbridge, but also the ecclesiastical parish of Huntspill. Much of its land is within the West Huntspill parish. There were of course many other farms and smallholdings, some of which have ceased farming only within the last 25 years, among them Greenwood and Sealey's. These and others still exist as private residences. Each, prior to modern farming methods, would have had a large workforce that would have made up a large part of the community.

## *Alstone Court Farm*

When Somerset County Council bought Alstone Court Farm as part of their plan for the proposed waste-tip site, Mr and Mrs Roy Loud took the tenancy and moved to Alstone Court Farm in September 1980. They had barely settled in when in December 1981 they were flooded! The farm extends to 256 acres and today is run as a sheep and beef enterprise. Mr Roy Loud has shown Simmental cattle since 1984 at many shows including the Royal Bath and West and Devon County. He has had successes at both events winning the Champion Bull in 1985 at the Devon County Show and the Champion Female in 1998 at both events with Taurus Jade Seventh. The cattle were shown by Mr Desmond March.

*Grove Farm field (the old cricket field) before Dutch elm disease struck in the late 1970s.*

## Farms

*Home Farm, Silver Street, with Mr Pearce, early-20th century.*

*Bert Rowe at Guy's Farm, 1930s.*

*Church Fête at Grove Farm.*

## Alstone Court Farm

*Alstone Court.*

*Alstone Court Farm prize-winning cattle at the Newbury Show, 1998.*
Left to right: *Desmond March, Gordon Difford and Roy Loud.*

The Louds began a successful bed-and-breakfast venture in 1983 and a year later Susan, the oldest daughter, started a riding stables. In 1988, Sally took over the reins of the school from her sister, when Susan married and moved away. Later Sally opened Riverside Tack Shop to supply the equestrian needs of the locality. The year 1995 saw Sally holding her first very successful Alstone Court Horse and Dog Charity Show, which has proved very popular as it pays particular attention to encouraging the less experienced rider and is renowned for its friendly atmosphere. Many local charities have benefited from the generosity of the show committee.

The history of the farmhouse dates back beyond 1715 when it was owned by a Mr Gatchell. The Poor Rate at that time shows a property of 92½ acres in his possession with an annual value of £66. By 1730 a Mr Janes of West Monkton had taken the farm over and the acreage gradually increased; as did its value to £67 in 1733. The Janes family held various properties in and around Huntspill, including at Mark Moor. In 1766 Mr Merchant of South Brent was the tenant and by 1829 Alstone was part of the estate of Alexander Baring. The property then passed to Lord Ashburton, with William Haines followed by William Tilley as the tenants.

During the successive changes various alterations and additions have been made to the original building and of course the size of the farm has also increased to that of its present acreage of 256. Closer to our time there is known to be a sales catalogue surviving from 1937.

Alstone Court Farm was in the tithing of Alstone Maris and is shown as Alstone Court on the Tithe Map of 1840. An earlier survey map of 1802 shows the spelling of Alstone as 'Arston'. Even earlier, the Somerset Quarter Sessions of 1673 mentions a case regarding sheep grazing on Alstone Warth.

## Brue Farm
### by Gordon Lockyer

We came to Brue Farm on Thursday 8 November 1962. On the following Saturday I went to Taunton Market and bought my first four cows. The milk lorry came on the Sunday morning and took the milk in churns to The Old Creamery in Huntspill Road. After about two years The Old Creamery closed and the milk, still in churns, went to Bason Bridge. I think it was around 1975 that I changed over to a bulk tank collection which came every day, but now collection is every other day. The most I milked was about 52 cows. I also had beef, sheep and pigs.

Linda was born in 1964, Austen in 1966 and then Graham in 1970. They all went to West Huntspill School. I started showing pigs in 1963 at Highbridge Market, and after that I showed cattle from 1965 to

1999. In 1967 all shows were cancelled as there was an outbreak of foot and mouth, the last big outbreak until 2001. In all I won eleven Champions and seven Reserves at Highbridge Market. I started going to the Royal Smithfield Show in 1977 and won many prizes. In 1985 and 1986 I won the Queen Mother's Cup for the Best Pure Breed with South Devons and I also had cattle in a team of three which won the Duke of Norfolk Cup three times.

About 52 years ago, when I was a young lad, we used to come to the Gymkhana and Pony Racing in the field behind the Post Office, the old cricket field, at West Huntspill. No hard hats or fancy boots were worn in those days, just wellies and soft caps. The Gas brothers used to run races in Highbridge and races were also run at East Huntspill. We used to keep racing ponies at the family farm at Shapwick. My favourite pony was White Socks who was very good. On one occasion after she had won, I returned to the box to find that my brothers had just sold her to a Mr Dennis Baker. I told them they could just 'un-sell' her. That was on the Saturday, we raced her again the next Sunday but she broke down and never raced again.

*Gordon Lockyer, Brue Farm, being presented with the Queen Mother's Cup at the Smithfield Show, 1985.*

*Gordon Lockyer, Brue Farm, being presented with the Queen Mother's Cup at the Smithfield Show, 1986.*

*Gordon Lockyer, Brue Farm, with his Highbridge Show Champion, 1976.*

## Court Farm

Court Farm is situated just off the main A38 adjoining Huntspill Court. The house is between 250 and 300 years old. Early records state that there was once a tunnel leading from the cellars of the Court to the farm. The house is built of stone and there is an archway of bricks at ground level perhaps indicating an access way to the cellars below. The 32-acre farm was owned by the Watts family from the early 1900s until it was sold in 1990. Harry and Florence worked the farm until Harry's early death in 1929 at the age of 47. His only son Wyndham continued the farm with the help of his uncle, Mr Hubert Rowe. Often he would walk to the sea wall to tend the sheep before going to school in the mornings and travel the same journey again in the evening. His mother died in 1937 and he was left to run the farm single-handed. He met his future wife Eva at the Highbridge Creamery where he used to go daily with the horse and cart to deliver the milk in 20-gallon churns. They married in 1938 and had their only holiday during their 58 years together, one night at Eva's home and then back to the farm! The farm reared mainly pigs and dairy cattle and Eva always enjoyed looking after the poultry.

Before electricity was installed in 1956, lighting for the house was provided by means of batteries charged up from a windmill. This was later replaced with a Petter engine which was also used to generate power for a milking machine and a 10-inch screen television. The engine also pumps water from the well in the garden which is still used daily and has never been known to run dry. Perhaps this is the only property in the village not connected to mains water.

Wyndham retired from milking in the 1980s and sold the farm to Jane and Tony Wadsworth in 1990 who are continuing the farming tradition breeding and showing cattle.

## Court Farm, West Huntspill
### by Tony and Jane Wadsworth

We purchased the farm, extending to 34 acres, from Mr and Mrs Wyndham Watts in November 1990 – the week of the demise of Mrs Thatcher. Mr and Mrs Watts had retired from a lifetime's farming and had moved to Church Road. They had sold their milking herd some years before. Mr Watts had left a few hens and visited daily, but by the time we arrived one hen only remained, the others having been taken by foxes. We named the survivor Maggie after Mrs Thatcher!

*Mr and Mrs Wyndham Watts at Court Farm, 1941.*

*Court Farm, 1940s.*

This was the realisation of Tony's dream to go into farming and build up a small pedigree beef herd. We have not made a profit, but Jane works full-time, so this outside income has supported us.

We chose the South Devon breed – large, light-brown cattle, known for their docility, and bought our first two heifers in March 1991 – Saffy and Flora. We still have Saffy, now aged 12, and she has given us nine calves and expects her tenth at the time of writing.

Our ten-year plan has extended to 20 years, God willing. We have modernised the ground floor of the house, which, we learned, was originally built c.1650 as the granary of Huntspill Court. We still have no mains water, but when the new main came through the A38 some years back we managed to get it connected to our first cattle trough!

We have replaced the old dairy with a utility room and shower, with the addition of a septic tank, and have a new garage in place of the lean-to. We have kept the brick-built south-facing cattle pens and built our own cattle housing and hay barns.

Half of the vegetable garden is now a fruit orchard and we have planted a variety of trees on the land. The farm remains all permanent pasture and our herd now numbers 37 cattle. We keep 24 hens and a pair of geese who have 9 goslings at the time of writing.

Apart from this year of the foot-and-mouth crisis, we have shown cattle in pedigree classes at shows in the South-West and also primestock shows at Highbridge, Taunton, Shepton and Frome. We have won prizes at most and our best success to date was to win Champion Bull at the South Devon Herd Book Society Autumn Show and Sale, Exeter, in 1994. He was born on the farm and named Court Farm Wyndham after Mr Watts and Jane's late godfather, Mr Cecil Wyndham King. He was sold as a breeding bull to a farm in Totnes.

Our hope is to stay as long as possible, trying to improve our little herd and hopefully enjoying future shows. Life for us in West Huntspill has been very happy, as we are sure it was for Wyndham and Eva Watts.

## Maundrils Farm

A stone bearing the date 1651 was discovered when some renovation work was being carried out at the farm and this would seem to indicate the year of construction. At least one family named Maundrell was living in the area in the middle of the 17th century. A Robert Maundrell was described in the Parish Registers as a 'Gent' so it may be assumed that he lived at the farm. However, a 1711 survey of landowners does not include any mention of the name Maundrell. There are many baptisms and burials of members of the Maundrell family recorded in the Parish Registers between 1654 and 1729 but surprisingly no record of any marriages. By the 1750s there were no Maundrells living in the area.

A map of 1776 shows Gould Esq. owning land on which the farm stands plus fields to the north, and a Mr Saunders owned land to the south. At the time of the Tithe Map of 1840, the property was owned by Henry Gould and occupied by John Jeffrey. The Jeffreys were classed as gentry in the village over several centuries and the 1851 Census shows John E. Jeffrey as farming 220 acres and employing six men. By 1861 his acreage was down to 160 and he was employing four men and two boys.

Ten years later in 1871 Clement Toogood, who was described as a farmer, farrier and, later, a veterinary surgeon, was living at Maundrils. By 1881 George Govett, a widower from Milton, was at the farm with his two daughters and a son, together with a nephew and a general domestic servant.

## *Maundrils Farm*

*Maundrils Farm, 1989.*

## PARTICULARS.

### Lot 1.

THE UNUSUALLY ATTRACTIVE GENTEEL

## Modern Residence

with sunny aspect, standing well back from the main road, and at convenient distance from the Farm Buildings, with spacious well Shrubbed Lawn in front and Fruit and Vegetable Garden at the side. The House has a pleasing elevation, handsome Stone Porch Entrance with Tessellated Floor; Spacious Hall, 25ft. oin. x 8ft. oin, also with Tessellated Floor; China Pantry, Wine Cupboard; Good Drawing Room about 14ft. x 15ft. 9in.; Fine Dining Room about 18ft. x 15ft. 10ins., each with handsome grate and mantelpiece. Front and back Staircases communicating with Landing, Five good Bedrooms, Cheese-room, and Lavatory. Large well-lighted Kitchen with modern range, Larder, Back Passage, capital Dairy, spacious outer Kitchen fitted with boiler, open fireplace, force pump and capacious soft water supply, &c.

At the rear of the house are Cider Cellar with Loft over, Open Shed, Coach-house and outside Lavatory.

There are RICK BARTON containing spacious Hay House. Range of

## Model Farm Buildings,

consisting of Calves House, 3-stall Stable, Cow Stall (for 20) open to the South, Barn, Chaff-house with Loft over, Wagon-house, other range of Stalling, Stabling, Sheds, Fowl-house and Yards, together with Valuable

### ORCHARD & PASTURE LANDS

in a ring fence, described as follows:

ESTATE OF MR. WALTER BOARD deceased

# HUNTSPILL, SOMERSET.

## PARTICULARS with PLAN

OF A VALUABLE

# FREEHOLD ESTATE,

COMPRISING

Genteel Modern Farm-house, Excellent Outbuildings, Highly Productive Orchard and Pasture Land, and Valuable Frontage to the Main Road,

AGGREGATING

## 81½ acres (or thereabouts),

AND KNOWN AS

## MAUNDRIL'S FARM

Situate in West Huntspill, in the Parish of Huntspill, in the occupation of Mr. Charles Fear,

In the Heart of the Dairying & Cheese-making Industry, close to the Important Market Town of HIGHBRIDGE,

Which will be Sold by Auction, by

## MARWOOD J. CROSS & CO.,

as the within-mentioned or such other Lots as may be determined at the time of Sale), and subject to Conditions of Sale, at THE RAILWAY HOTEL, HIGHBRIDGE, on TUESDAY, the 28th day of SEPTEMBER, 1915, at 2.30 p.m. sharp.

Orders to View, Particulars and Plans may be obtained at the Offices of the AUCTIONEERS, 15 High Street, Weston-super-Mare, or of

WM. SMITH & SONS, Solicitors,
WESTON-SUPER-MARE.

*Particulars of sale of Maundrils Farm for Tuesday 28 September 1915.*

## *Maundrils Farm*

*Hunt Master Richard Perry, Weston and Banwell Harriers, at Maundrils Farm, 1992.*

*Breeder Club Show at Maundrils Farm, 1989. Millhouse Farm is in the background.*

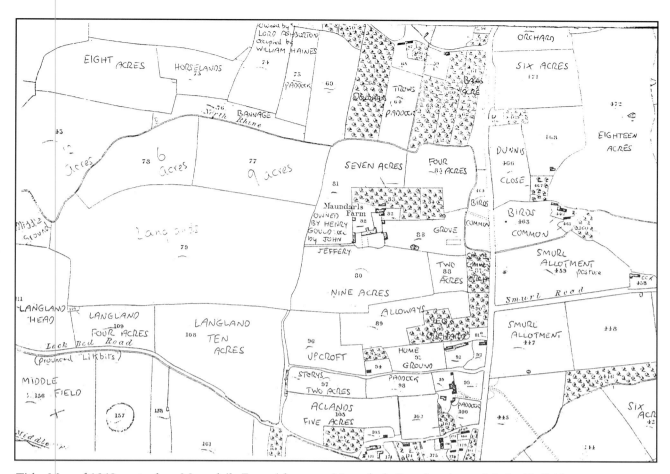

*Tithe Map of 1840 centred on Maundrils Farm (shown as Maundarls Farm) and annotated with field names.*

Part of the original stone farmhouse was re-built in the late-19th century. There are documents of May 1868 showing proposed alterations although this set of plans was apparently not used.

The farm's name appears to have changed over the years before it became Maundrils Farm. A survey map of 1802 records the farm as Arston Farm but at the time of the 1840 Tithe Map the name had become Maundarls. Variations in the spelling of the farm's present name have continued over the years until today's accepted spelling of Maundrils.

At the beginning of the 20th century in 1910, the Inland Revenue gave the owners and occupiers of Maundrils as Walter Board, Charles Brown and Charles Fear. A sale catalogue of 1915 for the estate of Mr Walter Board, deceased, described the property as a:

*... valuable FREEHOLD ESTATE comprising Genteel Modern Farm-House, Excellent Outbuildings, Highly Productive Orchard and Pasture Land, and Valuable Frontage to the Main Road, aggregating 81+ acres or thereabouts and known as Maundrils Farm.*

The catalogue also indicates that the farm was in the occupation of Mr Charles Fear. The auction would be at the Railway Hotel, Highbridge, on 'Tuesday the 28th day of September 1915 at 2.30pm sharp'. Interestingly the farm was described as being in the heart of the dairying and cheese-making industry, close to the important market town of Highbridge.

Mr Charles Fear went on to purchase the freehold of the farm from the estate of the late Mr Walter Board and continued to farm the whole of Maundrils until the early 1950s. Mr Reginald Watts of Poplar Farm then acquired the use of some of the grass and on the passing of Mr Fear in 1956 Mr Watts arranged to farm the whole of Maundrils Farm as a tenant with his four sons.

In 1959 Reginald Watts' second son David was married to Mary and they occupied the farmhouse, continuing as tenants until 1968 when they were able to purchase the freehold. In 1996 David and Mary's youngest daughter Rachel and her husband Joe became partners in the farm business, which has since traded as Maundrils Farm Partnership producing organic milk and lamb. With the demise of so many farms in the parish over the last 50 years, one can but hope that small family enterprises like this have a future in Britain.

# Plymor Hill Farm
## by Fred House

I was born at Plymor Hill Farm in 1928, where I lived for 60 years, my parents having moved in some years previous to 1928. My mother started taking 'paying guests', as they were known in those days, in 1935; then doing bed and breakfast with an evening meal until 1954. This was mainly to help keep the farm prosperous.

In 1942, a milk round was established as seen in the *Church Magazine* advertisement. My brother and a Land Girl from Devon covered all of West Huntspill with a pony and cart. The first two black and white pedigree cows were bought in 1943 from a farm at Locking. These were the first Friesian cows for miles around – otherwise all the other cows were Shorthorns. This was the start of the Plymor herd of pedigree Friesians.

The farm was all grass until the war when the Somerset War Agricultural Committee came and made us plough up virgin land to help feed the country. What a complete turn around now! The crops were mainly wheat, with big round stacks built and thatched waiting for the threshing machine. Now the farm is dairy, sheep and beef. Originally it was around 120 acres but has grown to 200 as other small farms gave up and land was bought. There are also 100 acres of rented grass.

The Huntspill River, which was created during the war to supply millions of gallons of water for the ROF factory at Puriton, cut the farm virtually in half and took many acres with it which now comprise the river and its banks.

My mother also made cheese. Miss K.D. Maddever, now with an OBE for her services to cheese-making, did her training at the farm before going on to Cannington College.

So as you can see a lot of history and happy times have been had at the farm and I hope will still continue with my son running the farm. I thank the Lord for my life, wife, family and farm.

Left: *Plymor Hill Farm, 1960s, with Mr and Mrs Fred House and Fred's cousin from Australia (on the left).*

Below: *Plymor Hill Farm, 1999.*

# Poplar Farm

Poplar Farm in Puriton Road, which is better known as Black Ditch, has been in the Watts family for three generations. The earliest date for the farm that has so far been found and recorded is 1839/40 although in all probability there was a house there before that date. In the records of 1839 the house was known as 'Late Sims House'.

Mr Herbert Watts bought the farm, then known as Puriton Road Farm, in 1907. In 1934 he entered into an agreement with his son Reg, whereby he became the landlord with Reg as the tenant. By now the holding had been renamed Poplar Farm. The following are some of the seemingly unusual conditions of the tenancy that the landlord required:

*To stack and consume on the said farm all the hay, fodder and all consumable produce grown thereon and to spread and bestow the manure made there on in an equitable manner on some part of the land every year at seasonable times and in the last year such manure to be left for the incoming tenant.*

*Not to mow the Orchard or Pasture at any time. Not to mow the meadow land nor any part thereof more than once in each alternate year and then in proper season. To cut the thistles, docks, rushes and other weeds before seeding. To kill and destroy moles and annually dig out ant batches and scatter moles hills. Not to stock the grass land with more than two horses at any time and generally manage the said holding with the view to the improvement thereof.*

*To keep the hay insured against fire to its full value and should the same be burnt to expend the amount received from the Insurance Company in respect thereof in the purchase of other feeding stuffs which shall be fed on the said lands, and such feeding stuffs shall be treated as in lieu of the hay destroyed and no claim shall be made in respect of the manurial value thereof.*

*To plant in the next season a thriving young apple tree of an approved sort in the place of any tree which may die or be blown down or damaged and fence and protect the same from injury and to leave the trees properly fenced and uninjured.*

The farm has always been a mixed farm and extends to 270 acres. There are now 120 milking cows which have all been reared on the farm – this being known as a closed herd. Dairy farming has always been important but this in combination with another enterprise. Today the farm is dairy and arable but until 1983 sheep were combined with the dairy herd.

*Poplar Farm, 1988.*

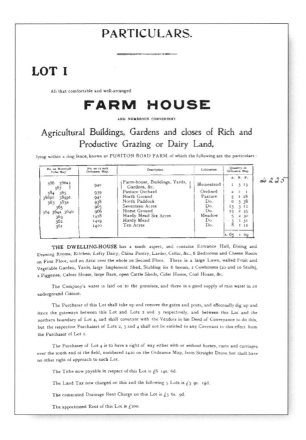

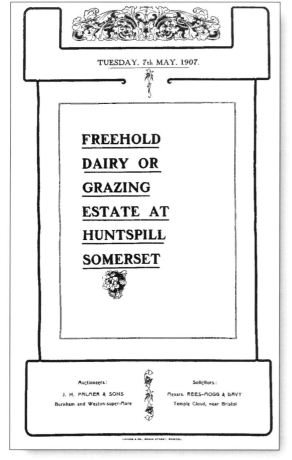

*Particulars of sale of Puriton Road Farm (later named Poplar Farm) for Tuesday 7 May 1907.*

A major change in the farm occurred in 1941 when the Huntspill River was cut for the Ordnance factory at Puriton. The river now cuts the farm in half, as the property runs between the A38 and Puriton Road.

Grandfather Watts had Berkeley House built on the corner of Puriton Road and Withy Road. The family, including Mr Reg Watts, father of Mr Brian Watts the present owner, lived there to start with before moving to Poplar Farm. In 1967 Mr Reg Watts and his son Brian farmed as a partnership. Later, in 1971/72, Brian and Ann Watts took over as the farming partnership.

# PUBS

The farmworkers, villagers and the travelling public on the turnpike highway, now the A38, would have taken refreshment in the public houses of the parish. The Royal Artillery, probably Victorian, is reputedly the only pub with this name in the country. It was so named in the early-20th century with the permission of the War Office. A brewery director, General Sir Charles Alfrey, named it after his own regiment. Interestingly the pub stands on Alstone Lane which was at some earlier date named Fackrells Lane. The Orchard Inn has become a public house only since the Second World War, having previously been a restaurant. The house was known as Sunny Lawn and stands on the corner of the A38 and Church Road, which was earlier known as Poorhouse Lane. This indicates the building's previous history as the Poorhouse. The Scarlet Pimpernel has only been so named for the past 25 years. Previously it was the Globe Inn, the Globe Hotel and at the beginning of the 20th century Wilsons Globe Hotel, when it was used for local auctions.

The Crossways Inn has claims to originate around the 17th century. Its situation would have made it a calling stage for coaches and carriages. Being adjacent to the Common, it would have been part of the scene of the fairs and animal markets which occurred there until the late-19th century. There is photographic evidence of hunts meeting there. At the time of writing, a marriage is due to take place at the pub across what is termed the 'chapel bar'. The historical whys and wherefores of a ceremony of this type are unknown. Mike Ronca, the present landlord, has just celebrated 25 years of ownership at Crossways.

The ditty on page 150 appeared in the *Huntspill News* during 1975. It was probably written after 1827. As the George is counted as a Huntspill inn this would suggest a date prior to the formation of the parish of Highbridge in the 1850s. A lapstone was a stone held in the lap to hammer leather on. The population then was about 1354 so thirsty souls were well catered for!

## *Pubs*

*Sunny Lawn – now the Orchard Inn. It was originally the site of the Poorhouse.*

*The Orchard Inn, formerly Sunny Lawn, 1999.*

## Pubs

*The Globe Hotel in the 1920s with the Forge attached.   This is now the Scarlet Pimpernel.*

*The Globe Hotel, 1930s.*

## Pubs

*The Globe Hotel, Forge and Methodist Chapel, late 1940s.*

*The Scarlet Pimpernel, formerly the Globe Hotel, 1999.*

## *Pubs*

*The Crossways Inn in 1907/08 looking towards Highbridge with the ilex tree in the background.*

*The Crossways before the First World War.*

## Pubs

*The Royal Artillery, 1950.*

*Church Road by the Orchard Inn during the flood of 1981.*

# The Lapstone Inn

Come lade and lassies, wise and witty,
And listen awhile unto this ditty,
Selling drink a Cobler think it no sin,
So he sets up the sign 'The Lapstone Inn'.

CHORUS

The policeman try, but it's all in vain,
To catch the Cobler at his game,
But with his stirrup and his awl
'The Lapstone Inn' outdo them all.

Now Public-houses we have plenty;
But 'The Lapstone Inn' keeps them all empty,
The Landlords all doth grumble and grin,
Their trade is all gone to 'The Lapstone Inn'.

CHORUS

The Blindman's Inn and the George is handy,
The latter is kept by Waxen S..n..d..y;
But if you want Cider, Ales, or Gin
Go to the Bye-shop, called 'The Lapstone Inn'.

CHORUS

Lovelock's Cross Way House, and Masters' Globe
Is situate after the Turnpike Road,
But if it's true, as the tag-rags sing,
They can't come up with 'The Lapstone Inn'.

CHORUS

At the 'Miller's Arms and the 'Fighting Cocks' too,
The lads and lassies used to go,
But now it's quite a different thing,
For they all do visit 'The Lapstone Inn'.

CHORUS

The Postman's Arms is new come out,
It's kept by Letter-carrier Stout,
But for him they say it's no good thing,
As he cannot touch 'The Lapstone Inn'.

CHORUS

At the 'Coach and Horses', for a lark,
They try to got it up to the mark,
Go where you will, the news doth ring,
There's nowhere like 'The Lapstone Inn'.

CHORUS

So now to conclude this little song,
As I don't intend to detain you long,
All over Huntspill now they sing,
We all are off to 'The Lapstone Inn'.

CHORUS

# Chapter Eleven
# LITERARY COMMENTS
# & CONNECTIONS

## SAMUEL TAYLOR COLERIDGE

Coleridge first visited Huntspill one hot August day in 1794. He was on his way to Nether Stowey to visit Henry Poole, a fellow student of Jesus College, Cambridge. Coleridge was following an unhurried route through the Mendips with his new friend Robert Southey of Balliol College, Oxford. The two friends had evolved a scheme known as Pantisocracy, their word for an ideal community where all would be equal, and were intending to emigrate to America. They had gained the interest of George Burnett of Swell House, Huntspill. Burnett was also acquainted with the Pooles of Nether Stowey, and Tom Poole had kindly given him a recommendation to Poole's cousin John Poole studying at Oxford, in preparation for Burnett's future entry into the Church.

At 18 Burnett was four years younger than Coleridge and two less than Southey, and he had just completed his first year at Oxford. His father, John Burnett, a well-to-do farmer, was filled with misgiving when he saw that George, his youngest

and brightest child, had veered off his chosen course of studying to be a clergyman. Burnett's fate was sealed when he struck up a friendship with Southey who was a radical and an atheist, and with Coleridge, who was bored with the rigours of university life.

While Coleridge was at Cambridge his rooms were very cold and damp, and to alleviate the effects of flu he took opium in the form of laudanum. Burnett began to model his behaviour and habits on his older friends. His liveliest contemporary at Huntspill had been James Jennings, son of a shopkeeper. Jennings also, at a later date, joined the London literary scene, and became an avid disciple of Coleridge. Jennings was envious of Burnett and expressed the view that university life was wasted on a farmer's son.

Burnett was a long way from agricultural concerns and his caring family at Huntspill, and it was during this time that he recoursed to following Coleridge's habit of taking opium. Coleridge and Southey knew that Burnett was not their intellectual equal, but he was a strong advocate of their cherished

Swell House, 1930s.

dreams of an ideal community. They welcomed Burnett's adoration of their genius with open arms.

At Stowey Coleridge and Southey established their historic association with Tom Poole, and from there returned to Bristol where both became engaged to sisters of the Fricker family. Burnett set his cap at Martha, another Fricker sister, but with no luck. The dream of Pantisocracy started to fade, leaving Burnett with a stifled ambition to become a clergyman, and the onset of opium addiction. Coleridge felt he could not forsake Burnett who, in 1795, went to live with the poet and his new wife at their College Street house in Bristol. Burnett became a kind of secretary to Coleridge, and relied on him entirely for his living. At the behest of Thomas Poole, Coleridge, with his wife Sarah and new son Hartley, moved to Nether Stowey in 1796. Burnett returned to Huntspill but continued to meet Coleridge and his friend Wordsworth at Alfoxton.

In 1797 Coleridge travelled to Bristol to borrow books from the library, but stopped off to see Burnett at Huntspill. This was one of many visits Coleridge made to Huntspill, and he usually stayed overnight at Swell House. Later when John Burnett moved house, he would stay at Ilex House. The young men were known for their noisy, boisterous evenings, and spinet music could be heard in surrounding farm-houses as it tinkled on the night air.

One evening, as Coleridge turned off the main turnpike road at Pawlett on his way to the 'Shoulder O'Mutton Inn' for a tankard of ale, he was accosted by an old woman from Huntspill. She started to gossip and informed Coleridge that the young master at Swell House had been ruined by 'a vile Jacobin by the name of Coleridge'. A bemused Coleridge questioned the old dame further, and

learnt that neighbours of Swell House had often been kept awake by drunken singing and laughing when this wicked intruder and his friends visited Master George. Bidding him adieu the old woman called over her shoulder, 'and mind you watch out for that vile Jacobin, Coleridge'.

Burnett became a drifter and sponged money off his friends for opium. In the late 1790s a series of calamities struck this family. After unsettled weather and high September tides, there had been a disastrous flood at Huntspill. The sea encroached poorly maintained sea walls and breached the wall at Steart. The River Parrett overflowed. Acres of farm-land as far off as Glastonbury were affected and John Burnett's land was under water, and this just a year after his eldest son John died in action at Gibraltar. Bereft of two sons John Burnett soon weakened and died and was buried in Huntspill churchyard.

Tom Poole, Southey and Coleridge continued to subsidise Burnett and in 1803 a Count Zamoyski invited him to be an English tutor and to stay in Poland for a while. On his return to England Burnett stayed at Huntspill for the last time and actually completed 'Selections from Milton', part of a serious study and a compilation of various writers' works.

According to James Jennings of Huntspill, Burnett's life was an indictment against educating people with humble backgrounds. Jennings wrote that his own jealousy of Burnett had been shared by Burnett's brothers and sisters. He wrote that Burnett might have been 'a respectable parish priest'. In 1811, adrift in London, Burnett made one last desperate plea to Coleridge for help but the poet did not receive the letter and later heard that on the freezing morning of 11 February Burnett had died in the Infirmary of Marylebone Workhouse. He had died thinking that

*Silver Street, late 1920s, by the entrance to Stoney Path.*

Coleridge had abandoned him. On hearing of his death Coleridge burst into tears for 'Poor, dear Burnett', and was filled with anguish that he had not received his plea. For a while the entwined destinies of Coleridge, the shining genius from Devon, and the satellite who was a clever local boy from Somerset, had merged in the light of hope, expectancy and promise. Addiction to opium had marred both their lives. The destinies of 'the star and the asteroid', as Jennings described them, had been irrevocably and for always entwined and had become an integral part of the history of a small Somerset village.

# FROM SILVER STREET TO BRITISH COLUMBIA

## A Lesser-known Huntspill Hero

In January 1856, a widower by the name of John Tout was married to Elizabeth Hill in West Huntspill Church. The 1861 Census shows the couple living in Town Lane, which was most probably the road running from the Crossways to the church. Ten years later the family were living in Silver Street and John was employed as a postman. One of their sons, Charles, was born on 28 August 1858, and was to become a noted anthropologist in British Columbia. It is not known how the family financed Charles' education at Oxford University, where he studied Divinity.

In 1884, Charles married Edith Mary Stothert, from a well-known Bath family, and adopted the surname of Hill-Tout (pronounced Hill-Too), which was a combination of his parents' names. Charles withdrew from University and with his family emigrated to Canada, where he farmed for a couple of years near Lake Ontario. Around 1889 the family moved to Vancouver where Charles was to become Principal of Whetham College. He was interested in the native Indian population and spent lengthy periods actually living with them, learning their language and making notes on their traditions. He excavated many of their 'middens' – ash and debris heaps which covered acres of land and could be up to 20 feet in depth, which revealed 2500 years of Indian settlements. Together with his two sons, Charles spent many hours digging for, examining and recording, relics, such as stone tools, burial cairns and totem poles. The results of these investigations were published in Canada and also in this country. Many of the specimens they discovered were later to be displayed in Canadian, American and European museums. In 1895 the Royal Anthropological Institute published Charles' writings on 'Later Prehistoric Man in British Columbia' which was the first account of the archaeological riches of the state.

The Institute went on to publish many of Charles' reports and in 1913 he was elected a Fellow of the Royal Society of Canada. In 1896 the family moved to a log cabin in what was to become the village of Abbotsford, close to the US border. Their pioneering experiences were recorded in a book written in the 1970s by their son James.

# MR GUY
## by James Jennings*

Mr. Guy war a gennelman
O' Huntspill, well knawn
As a grazier, a hirch one,
Wi' Ians o' hiz awn.

A oten went ta Lunnun.
His cattal vor ta zill
All tha hosses that a rawd
Niver minded badge or hill.

A war afeard o' naw one,
A niver made hiz will.
Like wither vawk, avaur a went
Hiz cattle vor to zill.

One time a'd bin ta Lunnun.
An zawld iz cattle well
A brought awa a power o' gawld,
As I've a hired tell.

As late at night a rawd along
All droo aii unket ood,
A ooman rawze vrom off tha groun',
An right avaur en stood.

She lookd za pittis. Mr. Guy
At once his hoss's pace
Stapt short a wonderin' how, at
night, She com'd in jitch a place.

A little trunk war in her hon
She zim'd var gwon wj' chile,
She ax'd en nif a'd take or up,
An cor er a vew mile.

Mr. Guy, a man o' veelin'
Vor a ooman in distress,
Then took or up behind en;
A cood'n do na less.

A corr'd er trunk avaur en
An' by hiz belt o' leather
A bid or hawld vast ; on tha rawd,
Athout much tak. together.

153

Not vur tha went avaur she gid
A whissle long an' long;
Wich Mr. Guy thought very strange;
Er voice too zimmed zo strong

She'd lost er dog, she zed; and than
Another whissle blawd,
That stortled Mr. Guy – a stapt
Hiz hoss upon that rawd.

Goo on, zed she; bit Mr. Guy
Zum rig heginned ta fear
Vor voices rawze upon tha win
An zim'd a comm' near.

Again they rawd along; again
She whissled. Mr. Guy
Whipt out hiz knife an' cut that belt,
Than pushed er off! Vor why?

That ooman he took up behine.
Begummers war a *man!*
Tha rubbers zaw as lad ther plots
Our grazier to trepan.

I sholl not slap ta tell what zed
The man in ooman's clawze:
Bit he, an' all o'm jist behine.
War what you mid suppawze.

Tha cuss, tha swaur, tha dreaten'd too.
An' ater Mr. Guy
Tha gallop'd all; 'twar ntver-tha~near
Hiz hoss along did vly..

Auver downs, droo dales away a went.
Twar da-light now amawst.
Till at an inn a stapt at last
Ta thenk what he'd a lost.

A lost ? why nothtn' hut hiz belt
A zuuimet moor ad gam'd
Thic little trunk a corr'd away.
It gawld galore contain'd.

Nif Mr. Guy war hirch avaur,
A now war hircher still
Tha plunder e' tha highwamen
Hi'z coffers went ta vill.

In safety Mr. Guy rawd whim
A ofen tawld that storry
To meet wi' jitch a rig myzel
I shood'n, soce be zorry.

* James Jennings was born in West Huntspill around 1750, where his father was the owner of the village shop. He spent most of his life in London but liked to write dialect poems, of which this is one. Legend has it that the money he acquired in the incident from the early 1700s enabled him to buy the farm in Church Road that still carries his name. Journeys as far as London were not lightly undertaken, hence the allusion to making a will before starting out.

# SOMERSET: THIS HOME OF MINE
*by Peter Derham**

New sun rising, misty dawn,
Sparkling dew on well kept lawn.
Cocks a' crowing, birds all chatter,
Farmer's wife and postman natter.
Tinkling bells from babbling brooks,
Raucous calls from big black rooks.
Morning light of subtle tone,
A new day born in this my home.

Mellow churches, brooding castles.
Lords and ladies, surfs and vassals.
Timeless landscapes, strong sea walls,
Gorge and moorland, rambling halls.
Humps and hollows, standing stones,
Land of sunset, ancient homes.
Tales and folklore full of mystery,
Wondrous deeds, dawn of history.

Country people, kind and shrewd,
Quick dry humour, never rude.
Sheep and pigs, dairy cattle,
Old stone farmhouse, full of chattel.
Grassy knoll and lofty peak,
Water meadows rest on peat.
Lakes and rivers born of streams,
Long hot summers, all a dream.

Waiting church, spring Sunday morn,
Slumbering folks wake and yawn.
Bells a' ringing, tall grey tower,
Hoar tho call, feel the power.
Village people strong and proud,
Lusty singing, soft and loud.
All in their way keep the faith,
Each to his own in time and space.

Shuffling feet, wood on leather,
Lush mown grass, balmy weather.
Batsmen, bowlers, fielders all
Slaves to no one, just the ball.
Players come and players go,
Umpire calls out yes or no.
Innings over, last decider,
Contest ends with beer and cider.

Glistening mud bank, autumn sun,
Churning waters seaward run.
Winter chills, tidal race,
Seasons changing at a pace.
Dunlins wheeling, changing hue,
Parret mixing with the Brue.
Drifting yachtsman homeward bound,
Home to Huntspill, hallowed ground.

Dancing snowflakes, gleaming white,
Ghostly shapes, a trick of light.
Silent mists, sharp morning frost,
Summers sleeping, nothing lost.
Roaring fires up chimney stack,
Keep us warm till spring is back.
Birds on wetland bide their time,
Till life's reborn, this home of mine.

---

*\* Peter is a Somerset man. His grandfather, born in North Curry, came to Huntspill in 1916, and the family has lived here ever since. Peter writes about the land he knows – Somerset, 'land of the sunset'.*

# IN PRAISE OF THE BALLIOL HALL
### by Marjorie Pengelly

At the Balliol Hall
We can all have a ball.
One can hire it for myriad uses,
Like the Welcome Club Tea,
Drama Group, P.C.C.,
Women's Institute, Clinic and 'Mooses'.

Yes, the Balliol Hall
Was designed for us all,
To abuse it would be such a pity;
So we all keep our cool
And obey every rule,
As laid down by John Davey's committee.

It's OUR Balliol Hall.
If the ceiling should fall
W'ell all turn out in force to repair it.
We admit it's the best,
When sufficiently pressed,
So let's loudly and proudly declare it!

# ON HUNTSPILL TOWER
### by John Keeble, 3 August 1827

Cove beyond cove, in faint and fainter line.
I trace the winding shore and dream I hear
The distant billows where they break and shine
On the dark isles. Around us far and dear,
The bright gay breeze is sweeping cheerily,
Chequering the green moor, like the summer field
of ocean, with the shadows of the sky
in all their graceful majesty revealed:
Now purble-shaded, now in playful light,
To south and north the glorious lulls are seen:
Where hovering fancy may at will alight
By pastoral dingle, or deep rocky screen.
Such airs, like sallies of thy cheerful heart,
A living joy, dear friend \*, to all impart.

---

*\* The 'dear friend' referred to in the last line was the then rector of Huntspill, Nöel Thomas Ellison.*

# HUNTSPILL
### Anon, 1977

A village is a lovesome place,
Full of kindness, full of grace.
With love and care for young and old.
Of bygone days many a tale is told!
Throughout our land these gems are found,
With ancient Church in hallowed ground;
The centre spot to hold most dear;
Our heritage from year to year.
Lord, let our lives in thankfulness
Be lived as worthy of this place.

# Conclusion

Our history has now been told, covering some 2000 years. A myriad of personal lifetime histories, from Walter de Douai via the Cogans, Jennings and Burnetts, to name but a few, to those of recent memory. The 21st century lies before us. What seems important to us today, will, no doubt, be irrelevant to the recorders of history in the next millennium. So it ever was and ever will be. Huntspill will continue as an individual community, the place and certain of its residents will continue to make an impression in the calendar of time. We would hope that all endeavours will be of benefit to our descendants.

*Stoney Path with St Peter's Church in the background, left. This is a church path which ran from East Huntspill. Once known as 'Corpse Path', it connected parishioners to the church prior to the establishment of East Huntspill's church.*

# Subscribers

Maureen and Nigel John Aish, Highbridge, Somerset
The Aish family, West Huntspill, Somerset
Sadie J. Avery (née Bird), Highbridge, Somerset
P. and L. Bamber, West Huntspill, Somerset
Carol and Richard Barnes, West Huntspill, Somerset
John and Dareen Berry, West Huntspill, Somerset
Denis Bird, West Huntspill, Somerset
Mrs Iris Bone, West Huntspill, Somerset
Jim Boon, Bristol
John Boon, Highbridge, Somerset
Michael Bowyer, The Grange, West Huntspill, Somerset
Marguerite Bowyer, The Grange, West Huntspill, Somerset
Diane P. Bray, West Huntspill, Somerset
Mr D. Brooks, Sloway Lane, West Huntspill, Somerset
Kelly and Wayne Brooks, Ringstone, West Huntspill, Somerset
Enid and Geoffrey Bryant, West Huntspill, Somerset
Nora K. Burrows, West Huntspill, Somerset
Burnett W. J. Case, Hemyock, Devon
Sara Chick, Braintree, Essex
Gordon and Sylvia Churchyard, Pawlett, Somerset
Mr Geoff Cole, West Huntspill, Somerset
Mary L. Coles (née Puddy)
Angela Cook (née Tippetts), Highbridge, Somerset
Dennis R. Cording, West Huntspill, Somerset
Josephine R. M. Coton, West Huntspill, Somerset
Amanda J. Counsell
Royston J. Cummins, West Huntspill, Somerset

William John Davey, West Huntspill, Somerset
Peter and Shirley Davey, East Huntspill, Somerset
Mrs Jean Davis, West Huntspill, Somerset
P. W. Denyer, Roamers Cottage, West Huntspill, Somerset
Peter and Barbara Derham, West Huntspill, Somerset
Christopher J. Derham, Weybridge, Surrey
Vincent H. Derham, West Huntspill, Somerset
Paul R. Derham, Boston Mass, USA
Julian R. Derham
Clive and Linda Dicker, West Huntspill, Somerset
A. J. and D. M. Difford, Burnham-On-Sea, Somerset
Marie Difford, Highbridge, Somerset
Mike Doble, West Huntspill, Somerset
Mary Draper (née Hooper), Highbridge, Somerset
Joyce Dunbavan, Highbridge, Somerset
Pansy L. L. Dyer, born West Huntspill, Somerset
David and Angela Evans, West Huntspill, Somerset
David, Vivian and Alex Evans, West Huntspill, Somerset
Paul Flux, West Huntspill, Somerset
Ian M. Frost, West Huntspill, Somerset
The Garner family, Honeysuckle Cottage, West Huntspill, Somerset
Mr Frederick Gass, West Huntspill, Somerset
Stephen Giggs, West Huntspill, Somerset
Mr and Mrs J. Good, West Huntspill, Somerset
Stanley Grant, Bridgwater, Somerset
P. M. Gray (née close), Burnham-On-Sea, Somerset

Tony Gurney, West Huntspill, Somerset
Brian J. Haggett, formerly of West Huntspill
Colin and Monica Hall, West Huntspill,
    Somerset
Michael J. Ham, West Huntspill, Somerset
Winston and Jean Hand, East Huntspill,
    Somerset
Sandra Hart, East Huntspill, Somerset
Ian and Anna Havercroft, West Huntspill,
    Somerset
Douglas Hewitt, Haresfield,
    West Huntspill, Somerset
Mr and Mrs A. Heywood,
    West Huntspill, Somerset
Jack Hobbs, Burnham-on-Sea
Stella Holley, Toronto, Canada
David and Violet Holley
John F. Holley
Michael J. Hopkins, Milverton, Somerset
F. W. House, West Huntspill, Somerset
Monica C. Huntley, The Langlands,
    West Huntspill, Somerset
Susan Hurford, West Huntspill, Somerset
Mrs A. R. Hynam, Brislington
Leo and Margaret Jack, West Huntspill,
    Somerset
Graham J. Jarvis, West Huntspill, Somerset
David L. Jenkins, Burnham-On-Sea,
    Somerset
Kathlyn V. and Allan E. T. Jones,
    West Huntspill, Somerset
Clive E. Jones, West Huntspill, Somerset
J. and A. Joyce, West Huntspill, Somerset
Patsy and Alan Kelsall,
    West Huntspill, Somerset
Heather J. Kerr-Peterson,
    West Huntspill, Somerset
Josie Kingsbury, Gresham Hotel,
    O'Connell Street, Dublin
D. Klein, Sloway Lane,
    West Huntspill, Somerset
Charles E. J. and Madge Langdon,
    West Huntspill, Somerset
Sarah Lee
Mr Trevor Lee, Old Pawlett Road,
    West Huntspill, Somerset
Trevor Colin and William Edward Lee,
    West Huntspill, Somerset
James Legg, Smurl Lane,
    West Huntspill, Somerset

Janice and Peter Legg, Smurl Lane,
    West Huntspill, Somerset
Peter J. Little, Burnham on Sea, Somerset
Mrs Janet Loney, East Huntspill, Somerset
J. and R. Major, West Huntspill, Somerset
Mrs Sylvia Marsh, Highbridge, Somerset
Shirley A. Martin, West Huntspill, Somerset
Paula F. J. McBride, West Huntspill,
    Somerset
Alana Miller, West Huntspill, Somerset
Ian and Jane Moreton, West Huntspill,
    Somerset
Ann Oakerbee, West Huntspill, Somerset
Adam Orchard, West Huntspill, Somerset
Terry and Ann Orchard,
    West Huntspill, Somerset
Jan and Don Ormesher,
    West Huntspill, Somerset
Mildred Ormesher,
    West Huntspill, Somerset
G. J. Parfitt
Colin Parish, West Huntspill, Somerset
Mr and Mrs Cliff Parkhouse,
    West Huntspill, Somerset
Mr William and Mrs M. Joyce Parsons,
    West Huntspill, Somerset
Richard J. Pope, West Huntspill, Somerset
Patricia Pope (née Inder),
    Highbridge, Somerset
Phyllis Preece, Bridgwater, Somerset
David J. Price, West Huntspill, Somerset
John Pritchard, West Huntspill, Somerset
Mr M. R. and Mrs A. M. Rawlings,
    West Huntspill, Somerset
Nicholas Reardon, West Huntspill, Somerset
Mr and Mrs D. J. H. and M. P. Redman
Martyn J. Roper, West Huntspill, Somerset
Mark E. Roper, West Huntspill, Somerset
Diana M. Roper, West Huntspill, Somerset
Maureen Rowe (nee Kingston),
    Taunton, Somerset
Valerie Rumble, West Huntspill, Somerset
Russ and Tom, West Huntspill, Somerset
Graham J. Saunders,
    West Huntspill, Somerset
Clare Sealey, West Huntspill, Somerset
Pauline and David Sly, New Road,
    West Huntspill, Somerset
Herbert Frank Solomon, born 1920,
    West Huntspill, Somerset

Leonard F. Speed, West Huntspill, Somerset
Jack and Joyce Tarrant, Alstone Lane,
    West Huntspill, Somerset
Sarah and Julian Taylor,
    West Huntspill, Somerset
Mrs I. A. V. Thomas,
    West Huntspill, Somerset
Mr and Mrs R. M. Tiley,
    West Huntspill, Somerset
Mr P. J. Tiley, Bristol
D. G. Timothy, Church House,
    West Huntspill, Somerset
Tony Tinniswood, Silver Street,
    West Huntspill, Somerset
K. J. Tolfree, West Huntspill, Somerset
Roy and Marjorie Tripp,
    West Huntspill, Somerset
Mr and Mrs D. G. A. Trott, Withy Villa,
    West Huntspill, Somerset
Roy and Liz Turner,
    West Huntspill, Somerset

Audrey and Roy Vickery,
    West Huntspill, Somerset
John F. W. Walling, Newton Abbot, Devon
Revd Geoffrey and Mrs Gloria Walsh
Michael and Pat Watts,
    West Huntspill, Somerset
Colin H. Watts, Burnham-On-Sea, Somerset
David J. Watts, West Huntspill, Somerset
Jenny L. Weeden, Burnham on Sea
Roger and Pauline West,
    West Huntspill, Somerset
Julie Williams, Highbridge, Somerset
Lydia Vera Williams, Highbridge, Somerset
Mr W. H. and Mrs B. Woolacott,
    Ringstone, Somerset
Marjorie Woolley, West Huntspill, Somerset
Bronwen and David Wright, Smurlands,
West Huntspill, Somerset
Joyce and Carol Young,
    Highbridge, Somerset
Beryl Young, Highbridge, Somerset

# ALSO AVAILABLE IN THE SERIES

# SOME OF THE MANY FORTHCOMING TITLES

For details of any of the above titles or if you are interested in writing your own community history, please contact: Community Histories Editor, Halsgrove House, Lower Moor Way, Tiverton Business Park, Tiverton, Devon EX16 6SS, England, e-mail: sales@halsgrove.com  If you are particularly interested in any of the images in this volume, it may be possible to supply a copy. Please telephone 01884 243242 for details.

*In order to include as many historic photographs as possible in this volume, a printed index is not included. However, the Community Histories are currently being indexed by Genuki. For further information and indexes to volumes in the series, please visit:*
*http://www.cs.ncl.ac.uk/genuki/DEV/indexingproject.html*